# Trans-Pennine Walk

## 54 miles from West Lancashire to Haworth

by
Richard Mackrory

Dalesman Books
1983

The Dalesman Publishing Company Ltd.,
Clapham, via Lancaster, LA2 8EB

First published 1983
© Richard Mackrory 1983
ISBN: 0 85206 746 1

*Cover photograph of the Pigeon Tower, Lever Park, by Michael Edwards.*

# Acknowledgements

I should like to thank David and Susan Storr for their help in the production of this booklet. Andrew Underdown, Philip Gilligan, David Shinn, Stephen and Maxine Maden deserve a mention for accompanying me on my walks. In addition I should like to thank all the members of local history and amenities societies who provided me with information about the walk and places of interest on the route.

— **Richard Mackrory**

Printed by Alf Smith & Co., Bradford.

# Introduction

LYING between the large industrial towns of Greater Manchester, Lancashire and West Yorkshire is the South Pennines. The landscape consists of wild, lonely moors, rocky gritstone edges overlooking steep-sided wooden cloughs and dells and industrial settlements occupying the valley bottoms. Although mills and moors dominate the popular conception of the area there is much else besides: fast-flowing streams, artificial lakes, old canals, ancient packhorse routes, colourful woodlands and towering railway viaducts. The Pennines have seen the influence of much human development in which the harsh environment has been shaped to suit man's needs. There are scars, but there is also considerable charm and beauty in some of man's works, particularly those which date from the beginnings of the industrial revolution and earlier. There are many places worth visiting and the most interesting way to discover the South Pennines is by foot. Strolls through the moorlands, valleys, towns and villages offer the best opportunity to appreciate the scenery, and that is the reason why I came to design a 54 mile walk across the region from west to east, using footpaths, bridleways and former packhorse routes.

The idea of a trans-Pennine footpath was first conceived when I was living in Manchester. Having enjoyed day-trips to Rivington Pike, Darwen Moor, Rossendale, Hebden Bridge and Haworth, it seemed a good idea to see if these points could be linked up by footpaths. Although the Pennine Way links the southern and northern Pennines there was no well established route across the Pennines from west to east. Looking at the relevant maps, however, there are a great variety of different paths, and it can be seen that such a route would be perfectly feasible. Using existing rights-of-way and commonly used routes, the walk from Adlington to Haworth was devised. Adlington makes a good starting point because of its location at the western extremes of the hills and also because it is well served by public transport. Haworth was selected as the end of the walk because it is at the eastern edge of the high moorlands where industrial West Yorkshire begins. Being in the heart of Bronte country there is much for the visitor to see there.

The route was planned with the following objectives in mind: (1) To cross the South Pennines from west to east; (2) to avoid large towns and cities, heavy industry and main roads, wherever possible; (3) to follow high ground and rural lowland for most of the walk; (4) to use established rights-of-way and commonly used routes; and (5) to visit some of the towers which form such a characteristic feature of the area.

The walk may be done either in a series of day walks, half-day rambles or short strolls.

## Equipment

Some parts of the walk can be muddy and boggy in wet weather and on those sections of the walk which cross high moorland the weather can be harsh. It is recommended that you wear, use or carry the following: a pair of stout boots, waterproof clothing, i.e. an anorak and overtrousers, a spare pullover, a compass, the relevant maps, a first aid kit, a whistle and emergency food rations.

## Maps

Most of the paths and tracks are distinct and visible and a few are signposted, but the route instructions and sketch maps should be used in conjunction with the appropriate Ordance Survey 1:50 000 or 1:25 000 maps. It is advisable to check your route against these maps from time to time to avoid wandering off the described route. The following maps cover the walk:

**1:50 000 maps:**
Sheet 103 Blackburn and Burnley (Sections 2, 5, 6, 8-11).
Sheet 104 Leeds and Bradford (Section 11).
Sheet 109 Manchester (Sections 1-8).
**1.:25 000 maps:**
Sheet SD61/71 Bolton (North) (Sections 1-5).
Sheet SD62/72 Blackburn (Sections 2 and 5).
Sheet SD81 Bury (Section 6).
Sheet SD82 Rawtenstall (Section 6).
'South Pennines' Outdoor Leisure Map (Sections 7-11).

The 'South Pennines' map is especially useful since it covers the whole of the walk from Whitworth to Haworth and it also contains additional information on leisure amenities.

## Accommodation

Overnight accommodation is scarce on the first half of the walk, although there is a hotel at Darwen and accommodation at the 'Strawbury Duck' Public House at Entwistle. In West Yorkshire accommodation is more plentiful. There are youth hostels at Mankinholes and Haworth. Further details from Y.H.A. National Office, Trevelyan House, St Albans, Herts, AL1 2DY. There are

# TRANS-PENNINE WALK: ADLINGTON TO HAWORTH

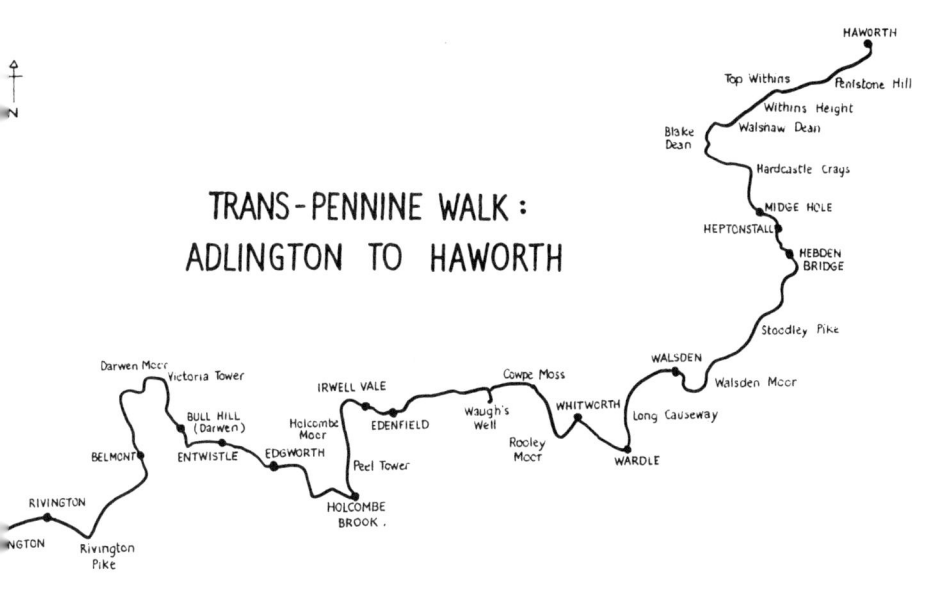

hotels, guest houses, inns and private houses offering accommodation in the Walsden, Hebden Bridge and Haworth areas. Addresses are given at the information centres below.

## Information

There are tourist information centres at the following places:

The Information Centre, 1, Bridge Gate, Hebden Bridge, West Yorkshire. (Telephone: Hebden Bridge 843831)

The Information Office, 2-4 West Lane, Haworth, Keighley, West Yorkshire. (Telephone: Haworth 42329)

These information offices are close to the route and are well worth visiting, because they stock an interesting range of literature and information on the South Pennine area. There are other information offices, which offer information regarding the West Pennine area:

The Town Hall, Bolton. (Telephone: Bolton 22311).

The Town Hall, Library St., Blackburn. (Telephone: Blackburn 52377).

Information Office, Piccadilly Gardens, Manchester,. (Telephone: Manchester 061-247-3713).

The Town Hall, Manchester. (Telephone: Manchester 061-236-3377).

The North-West Tourist Board, Last Drop Village, Hospital Rd., Bromley Cross, Bolton. (Telephone: Bolton 591511).

## Public Transport

Transport operators running services on or near the walk are listed below. Further details about destinations, service numbers, and times and frequencies of services may be obtained by writing to or telephoning the operators. The abbreviations used are those noted in the text.

**Trains**

| | |
|---|---|
| B.R. | British Rail, Information Office, Victoria Station, Manchester. Telephone: 061 832 8353. Stations at Adlington, Entwistle, Hebden Bridge. |
| K.W.V.R. | Keighley and Worth Valley Railway Ltd., Haworth Station, Keighley, West Yorkshire, BD22 8NJ. Telephone: Haworth 43629. |

**Buses:**

| | |
|---|---|
| G.M.T. | Greater Manchester Transport Executive, County Hall, Piccadilly Gardens, Manchester, M60 1HX. Telephone: 061 273 3322. Regular bus services to and from Adlington, Belmont, Edgworth, Holcombe Brook, Edenfield, Whitworth, Wardle. |
| R. | Ribble Motor Services Ltd., Frenchwood Avenue, Preston, Lancashire. Telephone: Preston 54754. Regular bus services to and from Adlington, Bull Hill, Darwen, Cadshaw, Holcombe Brook, Edenfield. |
| ROS. | Rossendale Borough Transport Department, 8, Bacup Road, Rawtenstall, Rossendale, BB4 7ND. Telephone: Rossendale 7777. Regular bus services to and from Holcombe Brook and Edenfield. |
| W.Y. | West Yorkshire Metro, Metro House, West Parade, Wakefield, WF1 1NS. Telephone: Wakefield 78234. Regular bus services to and from Walsden, Hebden Bridge, Heptonstall, Lee Wood, Peckett Well, and Haworth. |
| W.Y.R. | West Yorkshire Road Car Co. Ltd., P.O. Box 24, East Parade, Harrogate, North Yorkshire, HG1 5LS. Telephone: Harrogate 66061. Regular bus services to and from Haworth. |

## Section 1:  5½ miles

# Adlington to Belmont

THE first stage of the walk offers a pleasant stroll across farm pastures and country lanes to Rivington. The first ascent of the Pennines is relatively easy and involves a walk through the wooded parklands of Lever Park followed by a short climb to the top of Rivington Pike, an excellent viewpoint. Take a look at the two towers at Rivington before setting off across the West Pennine moors to Winter Hill, with its tall transmitter. There is a well defined track leading off the moors and descending into the village of Belmont.

## Route

The walk begins in Adlington village at the crossroads of the A673 Chorley Road and Babylon Lane by the Elephant and Castle public house. Walk along Babylon Lane for about 300 yards and when you come to a walled field on your right follow the public footpath sign along Greenhalgh Lane. Follow the path and turn right after 130 yards through a farmyard. The first view of the Pennines appears and the mound of Rivington Pike and behind it the television transmitter of Winter Hill may be seen. Climb over a stile and turn left along a metalled road. The road forms a footbridge over the M61 Manchester to Preston motorway. Thankfully the motorway is soon out of sight and earshot. When you come to a crossroads continue in the same direction along Horrobin Lane. Walk past a substation and the entrance to Home Farm. You will soon reach a causeway between Upper and Lower Rivington Reservoirs. There is another glimpse of Rivington Pike and the reservoirs have been well landscaped with trees to enhance the view. On the other side of the causeway it is not far to Rivington village. Walk past the school to the village green.

From the village green turn south and pass the Post Office and Mill Hill cottages on your left. Turn into the avenue leading to Rivington Hall Barn, which serves refreshments. Walk through the car park and turn right behind the barn so as to pass a cottage on your left. Enter the woodlands and walk uphill on a track keeping left at the first fork and going through a wooden kissing gate into a field. Continue to walk uphill until reaching a gate. You are now in Lever Park. After a short distance turn sharp left up a series of steps which twist and turn up the side of the hill, crossing Lever Bridge. If you peer over the edge you can see a rhododendron lined avenue. Turn left past an attractively landscaped pond with a view of the Pigeon Tower in the distance. Turn right when you come to another shelter, climbing a further set of steps until you reach the pigeon tower built by William Lever as a summer house. Turn right and walk along Georges Lane. Take the first left at the new toilet facilities and make the short climb to the top of Rivington Pike.

From the summit of Rivington Pike walk in a north-easterly direction towards the television transmitter at Winter Hill. At the bottom of the slope climb over a stile and walk over open moorland along a path, which crosses the River Douglas before ascending Winter Hill. After reaching the television transmitter turn left along a tarmac road, passing the iron monument known as Scotsman's Stump. Shortly afterwards when you come to the G.P.O. mast fork right and proceed downhill along a grassy track. In fine weather there is a picturesque view of Belmont village, church and reservoir. Further along the track at about the 1000 ft. (305m.) contour, fork left down an indistinct path, so as to cross a parallel track. Walk

## Section 1: ADLINGTON to BELMONT

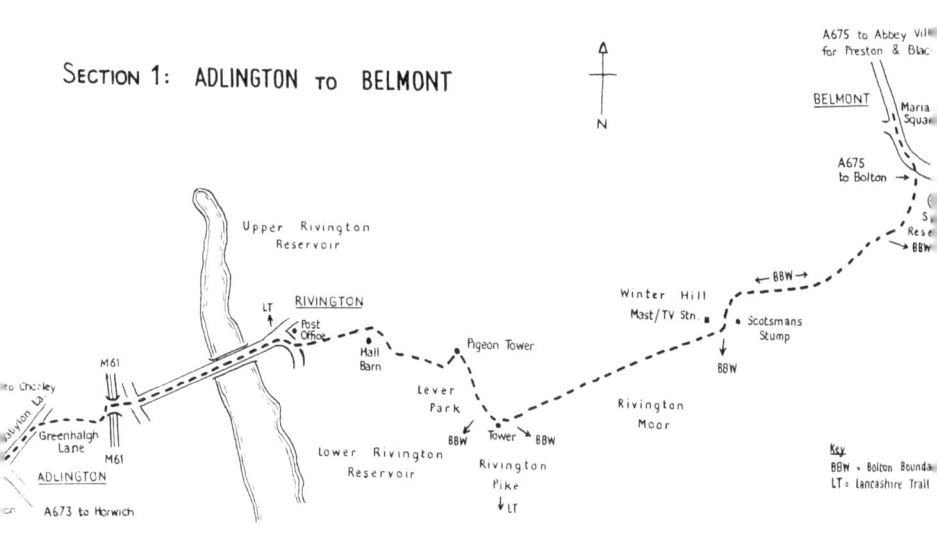

through the kissing gate into a field, walking in the general direction of Belmont chimney. Traverse the field with Spring Reservoir on your right. The path leads to the A675 Bolton to Blackburn road. At the stile a plaque, is dedicated to Mr. Harold Jones 'for his devoted duty and great work for ramblers'. Turn left along the road into Belmont village, where there are public houses, a post office and a general store.

## Points of Interest:

**Adlington.** Adlington contains a cafe open every day, shops, public houses and a W.C. There are also frequent bus services from Manchester, Bolton, Chorley and Preston (G.M.T. and R.). A weekday train service from the station runs between Manchester, Bolton, Chorley and Preston.

**Upper and Lower Rivington Reservoirs.** The reservoirs were constructed over one hundred years ago by Liverpool Corporation, and some parts of the old village of Rivington were drowned in order to build them.

**Rivington School.** Formerly the Free Grammar School of Queen Elizabeth, the School was founded by James Pilkington, Bishop of Durham in 1566. The discipline then was strict by todays standards and pupils were expected to rise at 5.30 am, for lessons at 6.0 which continued through until 6.0 in the evening. All lessons and conversations had to be conducted in Latin. The present building dates from 1714 and now houses a primary school. A tethering post may be seen in the playground as a reminder of the days when masters arrived on horseback.

**Rivington Anglican Church.** Richard Pilkington rebuilt the church in 1540. Inside there is a geneaological tree showing Richard Pilkington preaching at the pulpit in a painting above the north door. The church also possesses a 15th century chancel screen with a cornice of hanging tracery. In the churchyard is a detached bellhouse — unique in Lancashire.

**Rivington Unitarian Chapel.** The chapel was completed in 1703 and was Lancashire's first non-conformist place of worship. It contains a fine marble monument to Lord Willoughby of Parham. Another memorial records the ejection of Samuel Newton '... Driven from ye church on Bartholemew Sunday, 1662...', one of 67 Lancashire clergymen who refused to accept the Act of Uniformity which re-established the Church of England as an Episcopal Church.

**Rivington Hall Barn.** The barn is probably more than one thousand years old. It was extensively restored during the first few years of the century and is now used for dancing, wedding receptions, banquets, meetings and other community activities. Refreshments are served here every day.

**Rivington Hall.** The red brick Georgian style hall adjoins the barn and it originally belonged to the Pilkington family. Shrubs and trees had been planted to great advantage but despite the large number of trees to the east of the hall, no tree was planted to screen the view of the pike. Residents of the hall were able to receive signals from hunting parties when lunch was wanted on the pike. The hall passed to William Lever, Lord Leverhulme, the successful soap manufacturer who sought a property within easy reach of his business at Port Sunlight.

**Lever Park.** Lever Park was the creation of William Lever, Lord Leverhulme, who was born in Bolton in 1851 and rose from a humble background to become a leading soap manufacturer, philanthropist and world traveller. At work he was a stern master but there was another side to his character and in addition to building good housing accommodation for his workers he provided several public parks including Lever Park. The park was created to provide recreation for the townspeople of Bolton.

After completing the building of his residence, the bungalow, he was dining with King George V, Queen Mary and the Earl of Derby at Knowsley Hall, when he received news that Edith Rigby, a suffragette, had thrown a tin of paraffin at the bungalow and had set fire to it, as a protest against the way he spent his money. Lever, however, had been sympathetic to the cause of suffragettes at least up until that time!

Lever rebuilt the bungalow and lived there until his death in 1925. The hillside was transformed into a park with trees and shrubs to create avenues of honeysuckles, azaleas, rhododendrons and fir trees. Waterfalls and lakes were constructed and a number of shelters and a pigeon tower were built on the hillside. An open air zoo featuring wallabies, ostriches, llama and deer was opened. On the side of the reservoir Lever built a replica of Liverpool Castle. The park was opened to the public on 10th October 1911, but after his death the zoo closed and little was done to maintain the park. For many years the gardens were left to return to nature, whilst Lever's house, the bungalow, was demolished. Only recently has the park been restored to its former glory and it has now become a focal part of the new West Pennine Moors Recreational Park. Today the visitor can see the gardens and park in a similar state to that when Lever held garden parties at the beginning of the century.

**Rivington Pike.** Rivington Pike is 1184ft (361m) high and on a clear day offers an extensive view over the Peak District, Greater Manchester, the Lancashire plain and coast, Snowdonia, the Clwydian Hills and Lake District. There was an Armada Beacon lit on 19th July, 1588, and John Andrews built a tower on the top in 1733. The exact reason for building the tower is not clear. It may have been built to establish ownership of the moor, but it might have also been constructed purely as a shooting tower at a time when sham towers and pseudo-classical follies were in vogue. Fortunately, the tower has also been restored as part of the landscaping programme for the area. On the road up to the Pike some arrow setts may be seen. These stones were inserted into the road presumably as cart rests and to improve drainage.

**Winter Hill.** The summit of Winter Hill (just off the route) is 1496ft (456m) high. It can be seen from a long distance away by virtue of its television transmitter and masts. There is evidence of old disused coal, iron and lead mines and some shafts have been fenced off. Prehistoric burial mounds have also been discovered. Winter Hill has been the scene of five aeroplane crashes in the last 50 years. The most tragic crash occured in February 1958 when a Bristol 170 carrying motor traders from the Isle of Man to Manchester came down in deep snow near the transmitter. The first officer was wounded but managed to reach the television station and raise the alarm. With freezing temperatures, snow and visibility of less than 50 yards, helicopters could not be used in the rescue and only eight people survived the ordeal. The death toll was 35.

**Winter Hill Television Transmitter.** The television mast is one of the highest man-made structures in Britain and rises to a height of 1015ft (310m). The mast consists of a steel tube which is 9ft. in diameter at the base. When excavations were being made an unexpected difficulty arose when old coal mine galleries were discovered underground. Today four 55ft. concrete piles take the structure down to the bedrock. Other masts nearby belong to Lancashire Police and ambulance services and to the General Post for their radiophone service.

**Scotsman's Stump.** This iron monument near the transmitter was built to the memory of George Henderson, yet another victim of tragedy on the moors. It also marks a right-of-way. The inscription records the murder of Henderson and says: 'In memory of George Henderson, Traveller, Native of Annan, Dumfriesshire, who was barbarously murdered on Rivington Moor at Noonday, November 9th 1838, in the 20th year of his age.' Henderson was found dying from head wounds muttering, 'I am robbed, I am killed.' He never kept his appointment with a fellow

Scot he had arranged to meet in the 'Black Dog' at Belmont. On scanty evidence a man called Whittle was accused of the murder, but later acquitted and the real murderer was never brought to justice. For some years afterwards a Highlander played a lament on the moors on the anniversary of the crime.

**Belmont.** The village of Belmont grew up as a result of cotton manufacture, bleaching, dyeing and printing. There are several points of interest including the 'Independent Sabbath School' of 1852 and the Anglican Church (1850). Near the 'Black Dog' public house is a row of weavers' cottages known as Maria Square (1804) An ornate water trough was erected to commemorate Queen Victoria's Diamond Jubilee in 1897, and a water memorial records a victory for the village over Bolton Corporation in 1905. The corporation, owners of the nearby reservoir, were requested to allow compensation water to flow into a local stream for the benefit of the village. This protection was only won after a battle in the Houses of Parliament. It shows the strength of local pride in the face of opposition from the large towns. There is a bus service (G.M.T.) into Bolton from here.

## Section 2                                                                 6 miles

# Belmont to Bull Hill, Darwen

AFTER skirting around the southern end of the reservoir at Belmont follow a series of paths in a northerly direction to Lyons Den. Return to the moorland tops and walk across Darwen Moor to Victoria Tower, where on a clear day there is a good view of the textile towns of East Lancashire, and Winter Hill. From the tower walk along the edge of the moor to Bull Hill on the outskirts of Darwen.

## Route
Walk to the northern end of Belmont village and turn right to walk along the road at the southern edge of Belmont Reservoir. Leave the road and turn left after crossing the overflow/bridge. The track follows the eastern side of the reservoir for a short distance and then climbs a slope and turns away from the reservoir. At this point there is a fine retrospective view of Belmont and Winter Hill. Proceed to Higher Pasture Farm and go through a gate between the farmhouse and a barn. Go through another gate and bear left through some rough moorland, known as Pasture Houses Hey, keeping in a general northerly direction at a height of about 1000ft (305m). At the derelict Lower Pasture Farm fork left and walk on the right hand side of a mound known as Old Man's Hill. The path merges with a track, which comes in from the right. Follow the track for about half a mile until you reach the Tockholes road and sign.

## SECTION 2: BELMONT TO DARWEN Bull Hill

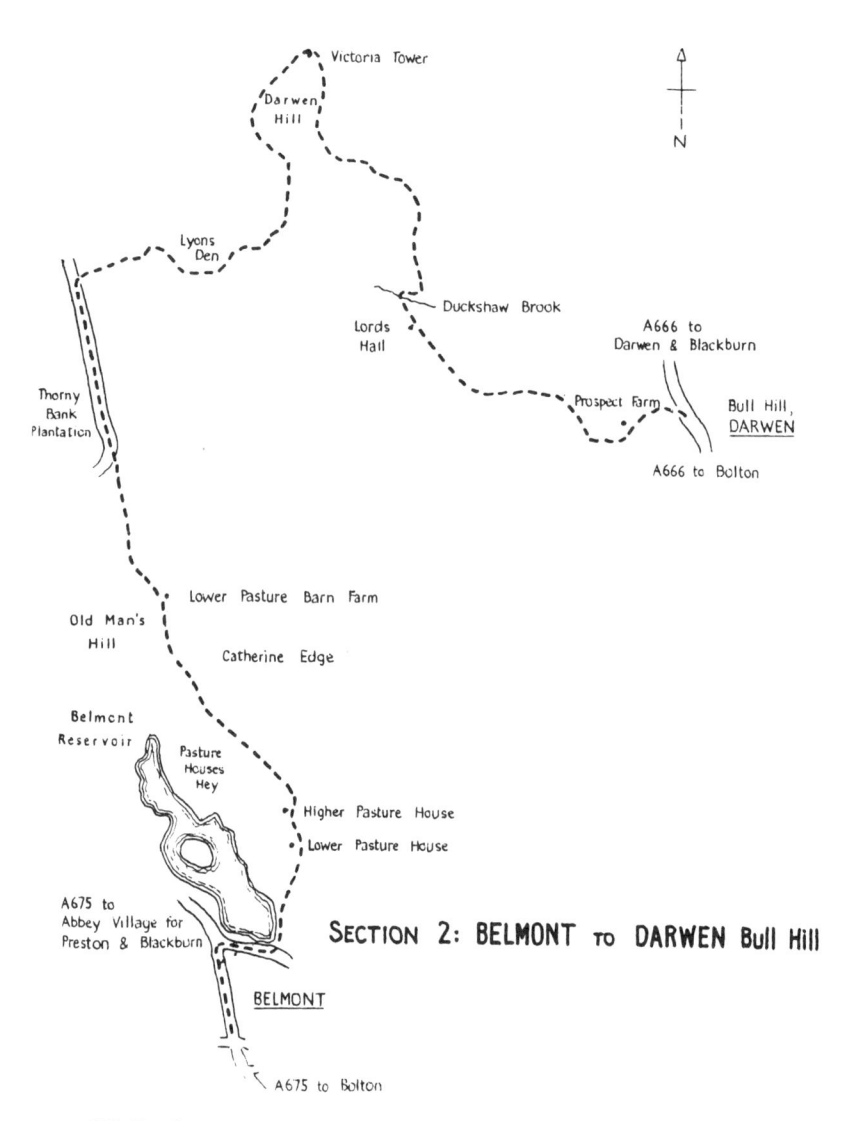

Walk along the road in a northerly direction past Thorny Bank plantation on your left. Soon you come to a signposted footpath marked: 'Lyons Den ¾ mile.' Leave the road and turn right to follow the footpath through Lyons Den. The path climbs up the slope and you reach a gate and stile. At the top of the slope there is another stile. At the summit the path forks into two separate paths. Take the path to the left and after about 40 yards turn left off the main path and walk in a northerly direction. Several seats have been provided for the weary traveller across the moor. Keep to the edge of the moor from where there is a glimpse of Victoria Tower, which later temporarily disappears from view. The path does not go directly to the tower, but instead follows the edge of the hill at a height of about 1220ft (372m). Ignore all the tracks downhill and follow a gravel track which leads uphill to the tower. A few yards away from the tower is an Ordnance Survey triangulation point.

Walk in a southerly direction from the tower along the edge of the plateau maintaining roughly the same height. After a while the path is joined by a track coming in from the right, but you should veer left here. At this point there is a fine retrospective view of the tower and a seat from which to admire the view. The path bends right, following a barbed wire fence and then a stone wall on your left. Next the path descends to meet a track above Duckshaw Brook. Turn right and follow the track uphill. The track turns left to cross the brook. Climb over a stile next to a gate and follow the track until it turns right to go up to a semi-detached building called Lord's Hall, strangely perched on the edge of the moors in an isolated setting.

Walk straight on along a grassy footpath continuing in a southerly direction. Climb over a stile and then walk over a small bridge. The path follows the boundary between pasture land and moorland, which is marked by wire fences and stone walls on your left. After climbing over another stile the path becomes indistinctive and then fades out. You soon come to a barbed wire fence and the field on the other side contains conifers. Turn right and walk uphill for a distance of 50 yards towards the corner of the fence. Climb over two stiles and turn left to follow the fence which marks the plantation boundary. Continue in a southerly direction until you meet a well defined farm track. Follow the farm track as it descends the slope, bending sharply to your left. It leads to a farmhouse called Prospect Farm. After passing the farm continue along the track to the A666 Bolton to Blackburn road at Bull Hill on the outskirts of Darwen.

## Points of Interest

**Belmont Reservoir.** The reservoir was originally constructed in 1826 to supply the needs of Bolton. In common with other reservoirs in the area its stone walls blend in well with the surrounding scenery. It has become a popular venue with sailing enthusiasts and yachts add colour to the water on summer weekends and holidays.

**Lyon's Den.** Lyon's Den is named after a seven feet high giant called John Lyon. Legend has it that Lyon was born in Westhoughton and that he built a simple dwelling using sods thatched with heather at this spot in about 1790. Three Darwen men, William Shorrock, Andrew Duxbury and Ralph Almond, went to investigate and found him crawling out of the low entrance to the sod hut and one shouted: 'See, he's coming out of the Lyon's Den.'

**Darwen Tower or Victoria Tower.** The tower is situated on Darwen Moor at a height of 1220ft (372m) and has an octagonal base supported by buttresses. The unusual shape looks remarkably like a rocket at a launching pad, when seen from a distance, although its real purpose was to commemorate the Diamond Jubilee of Queen Victoria in 1897. The townspeople of Darwen contributed towards its construction and a plaque records: 'The tower was erected and a sum of £650 devoted in aid of the nursing association of the public subscriptions raised to commemorate the Diamond Jubilee of Her Majesty Queen Victoria. Foundation laid June 22nd 1897 by Alexander Carus J.P. Esq. Mayor: Opened September 24th 1898 by the Rev. William Arthur Duckworth M.A. Lord of the Manor.'

Some 75 years later the tower was falling into decay and an appeal was made for its restoration. Fortunately the appeal was successful and a more recent plaque recording its restoration was unveiled by Councillor Dr. H. W. Lees, Mayor of Darwen. The stonework has been cleaned and windows inserted to protect visitors from the elements; 65 spiral stone steps and 16 iron steps lead to a viewing platform at the top of the tower. The view on a clear day extends as far as the Langdale Pikes in the Lake District, the Forest of Bowland, the Yorkshire Dales and the Ribble Estury.

The tower overlooks the town of Darwen, known locally as 'Darrun'. The huge India Mill chimney, modelled on the Campanile in Venice, dominates the town. The chimney is constructed of local Cadshaw stone. When the mill opened large scale celebrations took place. A local newspaper hailed the event as 'a new era in social history', when on May 7th 1868 the whole town was given a public holiday and an art exhibition was held at the mill. Oil paintings by Van Dyke, Claude, Durer, Teniers and other old masters were on show, as well as a collection of water colours considered by the 'Manchester Guardian' to be the equal of any ever displayed at the Royal Academy.

Darwen football club were early members of the football league and it can be claimed that they employed the first professional players. Another nineteenth century achievement was the development of a fine park called Bold Venture Park, where streams were converted into waterfalls and fine avenues of rhododendrons were made.

**Darwen Moor.** Many old coal mines and drifts can be seen on the moors. The area and neighbouring Tockholes were also used for nonconformist worship and illicit spirits were produced here. Lord's Hall on the eastern side of the moor was planned as a manor house, although this never materialised.

The moor was once the scene of a bitter dispute over public access in the 1870s and 1880s between landowners and ordinary townspeople. Strong feelings were aroused when the lord of the manor decided to deny the public the right of access to the moors. In response to this unpopular decision the move for freedom of the moorlands was initiated by John Oldman. He organised a mass tresspass, although only four walkers proceeded to walk across the disputed land, because of possible repercussions. One of the keepers, Richard Ainsworth, sided with Oldman and later joined the freedom movement. In July 1878 matters came to a head, when the men overpowered the keepers. On 1st August they were served with a writ to answer in the High Court in London the next day. Oldman was chosen to go to London, but had insufficient money. He obtained a loan on the security of a watch, walked to Bolton and then took the train to London, arriving in time for the proceedings. The court dismissed the application for an injunction and the court eventually decided in favour of the freedom movement, because the defendants had no intention of shooting on the moors. An agreement was later made to open some 25 acres as urban common and to allow the public to use all roads and footpaths. A procession of thousands climbed to the top of the moors on September 6th 1896 to celebrate the opening of the area to the public. In this case there was a happy ending to the battle of walkers' rights of access to the moors.

**Bull Hill, Darwen.** For those in need of refreshment a Little Chef restaurant is conveniently situated here. Bus services (R.) operate between Bolton, Darwen and Blackburn.

## Section 3    3½ miles

# Bull Hill, Darwen to Edgworth

RESERVOIRS dominate this lowland section of the walk which contrasts with the higher moorlands. After Cadshaw the route follows the banks of Entwistle Reservoir before reaching Entwistle station. The path descends to the banks of Wayoh Reservoir which have been reclaimed and extensively landscaped. A short stroll leads you into Edgworth village.

## Route

From the Little Chef restaurant turn right and walk in a southerly direction for 50 yards before taking the signposted footpath to your right. Two buildings are passed and the track bears left to run parallel to the A666 Bolton and Blackburn road. The track is overgrown and boggy but it improves as it merges with a farm track. After passing through two gates the track turns left to rejoin the A666 road at Cadshaw.

Turn left on the A666 road and travel 50 yards past Cadshaw farm. Take the first signposted turning on the right which is a waterworks track. Follow the track over the brow of the hill and take the first track to your right and go through a gate. This well defined track leads downhill in the direction of Entwistle Reservoir past some old

## Section 3: DARWEN Bull Hill to EDGWORTH

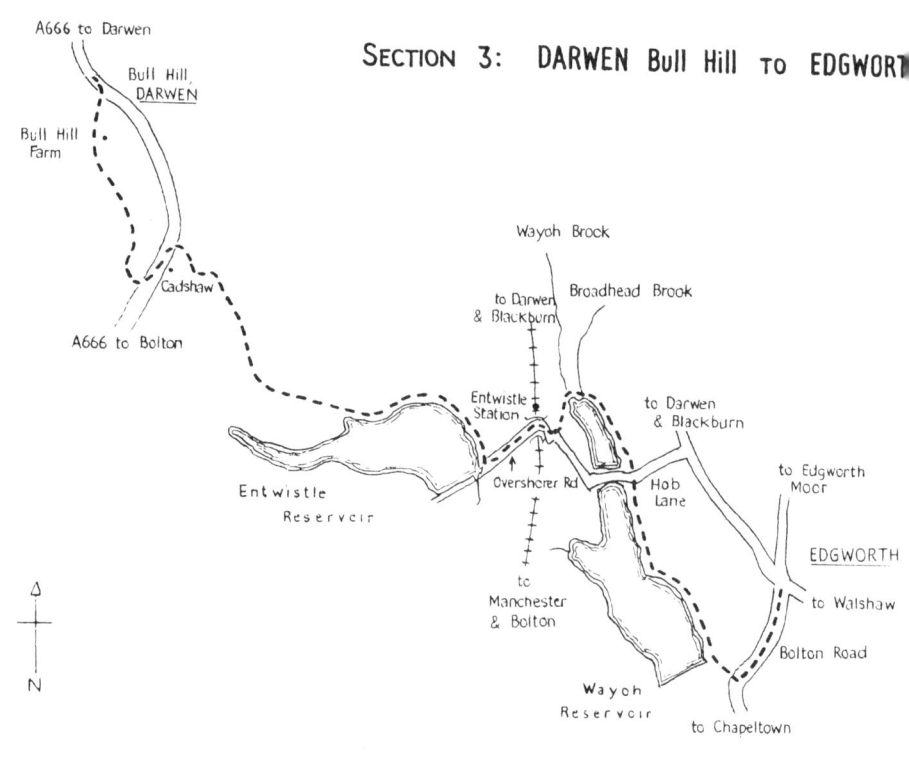

gateposts and the foundations of a derelict building. Climb over a stile at Overshores Road.

Turn left along Overshores Road, past some bungalows and terraced houses. After a short distance you come to Entwistle Station. Almost opposite is the 'Strawbury Duck' public house, which provides refreshments and accommodation. Cross the railway bridge and follow the road past Entwistle Kiosk Substation. Shortly afterwards there is a gap in the fence, where a path crosses a field. Climb over a stile and follow the path downhill to the valley bottom over two wooden bridges — above Wayoh Brook and Broadhead Brook. The path bears right to follow the banks of the Wayoh Reservoir. Further on is Hob Lane, a popular place for visitors during summer months.

Cross Hob Lane, go through a swing gate and continue walking on the track beside the reservoir. This part has been extensively reclaimed and landscaped following the closure of Edgworth Quarries. Continue in the same direction past the end of the reservoir through a car park belonging to the 'Black Bull' public house. Turn left at Bolton Road and walk along the road to the crossroads at Edgworth village, passing the Methodist Church, some cottages called Teapot Row, the old Wesleyan chapel (1828), the Barlow Institute and some playing fields.

## Points of Interest:

**Cadshaw.** Cadshaw Rocks (Fairy Rocks) are popular with rock climbers and offer a good selection of climbs. The cliff is natural gritstone formed by faulting and earth slips. One climbing handbook offers a salutory warning about the instability of the buttress above the mineshaft and suggests that climbers 'should bear this in mind and possibly take out insurance'.

**Entwistle Reservoir and Wayoh Reservoirs.** These beautifully landscaped reservoirs are frequently visited and plans are being made to extend recreational facilities for visitors. Entwistle possesses a railway station on the Manchester, Bolton and Blackburn line. John Wesley once stayed at a farmhouse at Entwistle.

**Edgworth.** Situated around an old Roman road from Manchester to Ribchester. It used to be a hamlet of scattered folds separated by rough meadowland although nowadays this meadowland has been used to provide modern accommodation for a growing population. Bolton Road leads to the centre of the village passing the stone cottages of Teapot Row and Kettle Row. Adjacent to the road stands Brandwood Fold, birthplace of Sir Thomas Barlow, physician to Queen Victoria, King Edward VII and King George V. A plaque on the side of the house reveals the villagers' pride in his achievement. The Barlow family erected the village institute in 1909 and helped to establish the children's home to the north of the village. One former pupil of the home is the actress Shirley Ann Field.

Today, Edgworth attracts many visitors because of its rural location, but alas Broadhead Youth Hostel at Pasture Gate Farm is no longer open. Edgworth does, however, offer a post office, fish and chip shop, food shops and public houses. Bus services operate to Bolton and Bury (G.M.T.).

Section 4                                                                 3 miles

# Edgworth to Holcombe Brook

THE route from Edgworth to Holcombe Brook continues across flat terrain through farm lanes and meadows. You are reminded that industrial Greater Manchester is not far away, but at least this section remains comparatively unspoilt. There are views of the nearby hills, but alas the existence of Holcombe Training Camp with its firing ranges means that this lowland route is preferable to one across the hills.

## Route
From Edgworth cross roads turn right along Bury Road and walk past the 'White Horse' public house and a bus stop. Walk down the left

side of 'Rose and Crown, public house and go through a gate to follow a track. After passing a caravan site and a cottage, ascend the slope towards Heyhead Cottage and Farm. Go through a gate and walk along a path above a stream on your right. Walk under an electricity transmission line, descend to meet and cross the stream, and walk uphill following an old field boundary path for a short distance until you reach the fence. Turn left and 25 yards further on is a stile. When you come to the farm lane to New Heys Farm, turn left along the farm lane in the opposite direction to the farm. Take the first track on the right which goes to Red Earth Farm.

There is no clearly defined path for a short distance beyond Red Earth Farm, so care should be taken to avoid straying off the route. Walk past the farm buildings and turn right to walk behind the buildings. Look for the entrance to a field just beyond their furthest corner. Walk in a north easterly direction, crossing the first field and pass through a gate. Bear left and walk into the second field. At the top of the second field turn right to follow a path which crosses the main stream marking the boundary between Lancashire and Greater Manchester. Make sure that you walk to the highest point of the field, otherwise you will be unable to locate the path and will have difficulty in fording the stream. The path goes through a gap stile and a gate to an old barn. Join the farm track near Lower Grainings Farm and walk in an easterly direction following the walled track. On your right there is a small wayside shrine to Roger Worthington.

From the walled track take the first turning on the right (Hawkshaw Lane). It is necessary to turn south here to avoid the hazards of the rifle ranges at Holcombe Training Camp. Walk past Boardmans Farm, dated 1707, past the lane to Withins and Higher Ash Farm. Walk under the electricity transmission line and continue past a bunglow and another farmhouse. When you come to a crossroads turn left and follow the track to New Hoyles Farm. Walk between the farm house and dairy. Go through a gate, walk along a track to another gate and cross a stream on a wooden sleeper bridge. Walk over the nearby stile and walk in a southerly direction through a field, following a fence on your right. Go over another stile and walk through another field following a hedge. When you come to a gate again follow a hedge. Soon you come to a pond, and keeping to the right of the pond use the stile in the hedge. Keeping the hedge to your left here, follow a path which goes under the electricity transmission line and go through a gap stile.

Walk through a kissing gate to a metalled road which is the road from the A676 to Holcombe Training Camp. Turn right on the road and almost immediately turn left over a stile. Walk across a field bordered by a stream (not marked on the 'Manchester' sheet). Climb over a stile and shortly afterwards turn left to cross the stream using an old wooden bridge. Walk uphill in a northerly direction towards

## Section 4: Edgworth to Holcombe Brook

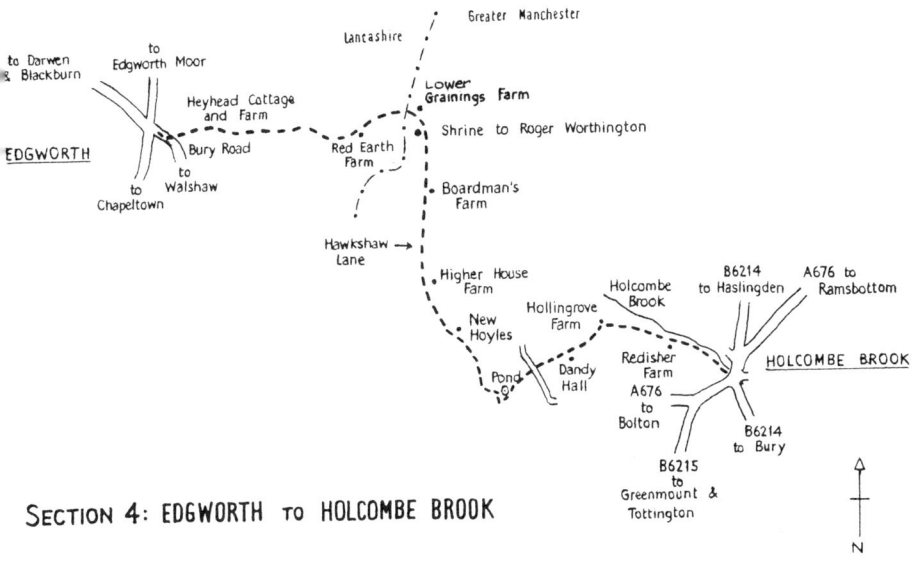

Dandy Hall. Turn right and go over a stile to the farm lane behind the farmhouse. The lane leads to another farmhouse and when you reach it, walk between the outbuildings and turn right to walk in an easterly direction.

On your left is the wooded valley of Holcombe Brook, and the route runs roughly parallel to the brook until reaching the village of Holcombe Brook. Walk along the lane which later turns right at Redisher Farm. The route turns left at the farm and passes through some woods above the brook. The beauty of the woods is short-lived, for further down the valley a factory has been situated. The path ascends the slope away from the valley to emerge by a row of terraced houses at Park Road. The road joins the A676 Bolton Road at Holcombe Brook, where there are shops, a public house and bus services.

## Points of Interest

**Shrine to Roger Worthington.** The wayside shrine to Roger Worthington, an early nonconformist preacher, is situated near Lower Graining Farm. The inscription requests that visitors observe this sacred spot and records the following: 'Here lies the body of Roger Worthington who departed this life the 9th day of July 1790 about the 50th year of his age. They that serve Christ in faith and love shall ever reign with him above.' It is said that Worthington was the son of a Roman Catholic family, but was disinherited by his parents on his conversion to the protestant faith. He became a hermit and preached to a small faithful flock in the hills. His final wish was to die alone and to be buried in this remote location. The original gravestone was broken when a horse stumbled against it but in 1934 a committee restored the site and built a small garden of remembrance and a year later Godfrey Ramsbottom, a native of Levin, New Zealand donated a stone which now stands next to the original tombstone.

**Holcombe Brook.** This is both the name of the stream originating on Holcombe Moor and a community on the outskirts of Bury. It once boasted a railway service and a trolleybus service. Ramsbottom Council was one of the first operators of trolleybuses, since they had failed to obtain trams. These vehicles started operation during August 1913 on the service between Holcombe Brook station and Edenfield, a distance of three miles. The system ceased on 31st March 1931. Today there is a good bus service to Bolton, Bury, Rossendale and surrounding areas (G.M.T. and R.). Bury Metropolitan District Council have devised the Holcombe Historical Trail which offers a short circular walk through the settlement.

## Section 5  4½ miles

# Holcombe Brook to Edenfield

THE short climb from Holcombe Brook to Peel Tower is well rewarded on a clear day with good views. It is an easy walk along the moorland edges. Following the descent into the Irwell valley the route passes the old industrial village at Irwell Vale before proceeding to Edenfield.

### Route

Walk past the 'Hare and Hounds' public house and immediately turn left along a tarmac road to a signposted bridleway — Holcombe Old Road. Climb uphill and pass a house on your left and several other cottages, until you reach a metalled road. Turn left up the hill past Gate House and a substation. Turn right along another metalled road for a short distance and then turn left through a kissing gate. Walk across a field in the direction of Peel Tower, which can be seen at the top of the field and walk to the summit using the well defined track. At the top is a view of the appropriately named Top of th' Hill Farm to the left and Peel Tower to the right, Walk towards the tower, which is a popular local viewpoint.

From the tower walk along a wide track in a northerly direction. After going through a gate follow the track to a crossroads of tracks and continue across in a northerly direction. The track goes past a farmhouse (Higher Tops) on your right and under an electricity transmission line. Go through a gate and past Chatterton Close on your left, which is supported by buttresses. Walk along the walled

## SECTION 5: HOLCOMBE BROOK TO EDENFIELD

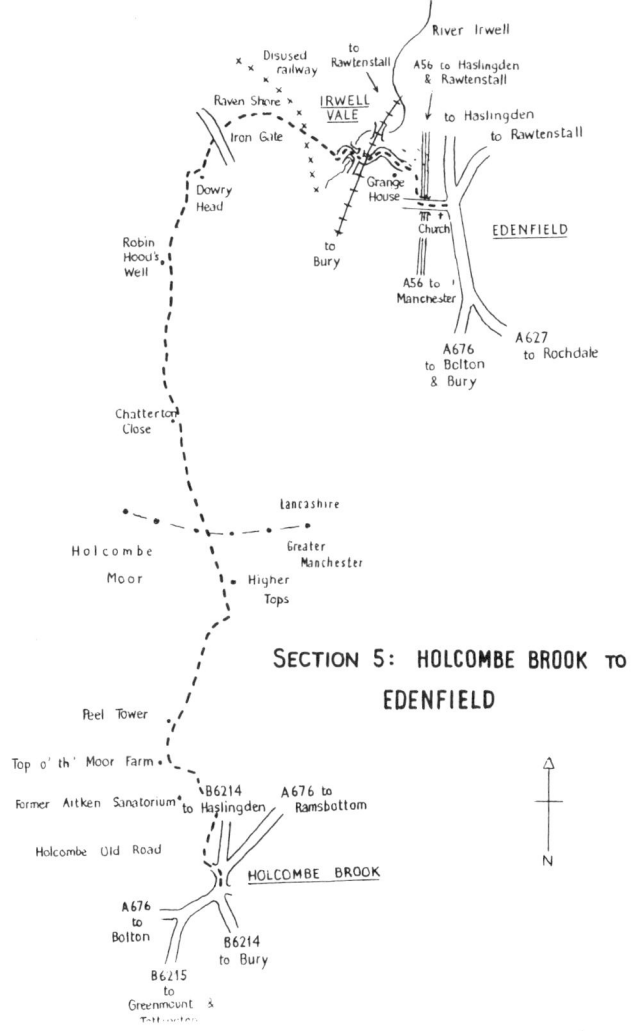

track and go through another gate before passing a wooden coppice on your right and the remains of old coal workings on your left.

Continuing in the same direction, go through a gate and walk along a walled track which starts to descend into the valley. On your left is Robin Hood's Well, an old spring. At the bottom of the slope the track comes out at the metalled road to Dowry Head. Turn right and go through a gate into a field. Walk parallel to the drive of Dowry Head for about 10 yards before walking diagonally across the field in the direction of a row of terraced cottages at Iron Gate.

Walk over a stile and past a hut before crossing the B6214 Holcombe to Haslingden road. After passing the cottages turn right along the track to Irwell Vale. There are a series of gates and a barn and bungalow are passed at Raven Shore. Walk over a stile and through a gate and then go over the bridge under which the Bury to Accrington railway line used to run. The track descends to the industrial village of Irwell Vale, now listed as a conservation area. After passing the Methodist Church, turn left into Bowker Street: a street with traditionally-built terraced cottages on both sides, constucted in the finest northern style. At the end of the street, turn right into Aitken Street and walk across the bridge over the River Irwell. Walk past the village store and you come to a small roundabout.

Turn right at the roundabout and almost immediately turn left over a railway level crossing on the former Manchester, Bury, Rawtenstall and Bacup line. Ascending the slope out of the Irwell Valley, walk along Hardsough Road past two rows of terraced cottages and Grange House on your right. At the top of the slope you arrive at the side of the A56 Manchester and Rossendale Road — the Edenfield by-pass. Turn right and go through a gate to walk parallel to the road for a short distance. Go through two more gates and continue in the same southerly direction until you come to a foot-bridge across the by-pass. On the other side of the footbridge walk along Church Lane past Edenfield church on your right and continue until you reach the road at Edenfield village, where there are shops and bus services.

## Points of Interest

**Holcombe Old Road and former Aitken Sanitorium.** Holcombe Old Road was the original coach road from Bury to Haslingden and beyond. Local authorities plan to put a sandstone sett surface along the full length of the roadway as part of enhancement work in the Holcombe conservation area. The Holcombe Historic Trail follows this route. On the left the former Aitken Sanitorium can be seen. This is an early Victorian high gabled stone and slate building dating from 1846. In 1974 it was acquired for use as an Islamic training centre.

**Peel Tower.** The tower was built to the memory of Sir Robert Peel, a local man, born in Bury in 1788. Peel helped to form the Metropolitan Police Force, the first proper force in Britain. He was also instrumental in repealing the corn laws, which caused grave hardship among cotton operatives. The tower was erected in 1851 by public subscription at a cost of £1,000. It is built from millstone grit quarried around its base and stands 128ft high on Holcombe Moor at 1100ft (335m) above sea-level.

The location of the monument was influenced by the merchant William Grant and it was positioned to be in line with St. Andrew's Church tower, Ramsbottom, when viewed from the doorstep of his home at Nuttall Hall (now demolished). There is an extensive view on a clear day. The remains of Grant's Tower may be seen across the valley and Ramsbottom, Haslingden, Bury and Manchester are also visible. On a fine day the faint outlines of the Yorkshire Dales and Pendle Hill may also be seen. There are plans to renovate Peel Tower, restore the staircase and re-open the building to the public.

**Holcombe Moor.** Two places of interest which are off the route are the remains of the Pilgrim's Cross and the cairn erected to the memory of Ellen Strange. The Pilgrim's Cross is situated on an old travelling route used by pilgrims going to Whalley Abbey and the original cross dated from 1176. Only the socket stone remained until this was badly vandalised in 1901. The 'Bury Times' referred to the act of vandalism as being yet another part of the problem of twentieth century vandalism', showing that it is hardly a new problem. Reverend Dowsett, who wrote several interesting articles and books about the district, was there to consecrate a memorial stone on 31st May 1902.

Further north, on the slopes of Bull Hill to the west of Robin Hood's Well, is the cairn erected to the memory of Ellen Strange. Ellen was an Edgworth girl who was the victim of a savage murder in about 1735. She became attached to a pedlar named Billy from Stonefold and they left her home at Ash Farm, Edgworth, to go to Haslingden Fair. They were last seen at the 'White Horse' Hotel in Helmshore, but later Ellen was found murdered on the moors. In this case the pedlar was arrested and brought to justice for committing this dark deed. He confessed his guilt at Lancaster Assizes and was gibbeted on Bull Hill. Local people remembered the spot where poor Ellen was murdered by erecting a cairn.

Holcombe Moor was once a royal forest and the haunt of a pack of hunters known as the 'Holcombe Harriers', who were given the right to wear the King's scarlet livery and to hunt the forest for ever by King James I of England in 1617. A few years later during the civil war some royalist soldiers camped in these hills.

**Robin Hood's Well.** The Well is situated on the left hand side of the track leading from the moors to the Rossendale Valley. It is an old spring marked by a stone and according to B.T. Barton in his "History of Bury' the probable explanation of the name lies in an out-of-door pageant, held in commemoration of Robin Hood.

**Irwell Vale.** This industrial village is situated on the banks of the River Irwell, which originally supplied power for the mill. The river is vastly different from the polluted river it later becomes when it flows through Salford and Manchester. At this point it is a small, meandering stream flowing through mainly rural scenery.

The main features of interest in the village include the Methodist Chapel; Bowker Street, a narrow street with traditional mill cottages on both sides; Aitken Street, named after the mill owners; the sign showing the Aitken coat of arms with a knight holding a cross: and the old Primitive Methodist Chapel frontage, which has been thoughtfully converted into three homes.

There are two old railway lines running on either side of the village. The Bury to Accrington railway was started in 1845 and once transported textiles and passengers between Burnley, Accrington, Rossendale and Bury. The line closed in 1960. On the other side of the village is the Bury, Rawtenstall and Bacup railway line. The line was opened between Bury and Rawtenstall on 28th September 1846, but has not carried passengers since 5th June 1972. The East Lancashire Railway Preservation Society have appealed for funds to purchase the line and they hope to run passenger services between Bury and Rawtenstall.

**Higher Mill Museum, Holcombe Road, Helmshore** (approx. one mile off the route). Although the mill is situated off the route it is well worth a visit. Higher Mill was one of Rossendale's first fulling mills and contains fulling stocks, a tenter frame, a fire engine and a water wheel, as well as other old machinery.

**Edenfield.** Contains shops, public houses and a fish and chip cafe. There are good bus sevices to Bolton, Bury and Rochdale, other parts of Rossendale, Accrington, Burnley, Preston and Manchester (G.M.T., R. and ROS.). Edenfield Church is a simple structure, built in local stone and dating, from 1778. It has a sundial on one of its walls. The inscriptions on the stones in the graveyard are well preserved and worth looking at. One poetic inscription is to Samuel Platt, a gravedigger: 'The graves around for many a year were dug by him who slumbers here; Till worn with age, he dropp'd his spade, and in this dust his body is laid.'

Section 6                                                                6½ miles

# Edenfield to Whitworth (Tonacliffe)

THE walk over the empty moorlands between Edenfield and Whitworth is certainly 'off the beaten track' and few tourists visit the area. There is a wealth of industrial remains including remnants of old railway lines, old packhorse routes and quarries. The presence of stone flags from the quarries facilitates walking even during wet weather! After leaving the moorlands the route descends to cross Healey Dell before reaching Tonacliffe, a suburb of Whitworth.

## Route

From the main street in Edenfield take the signposted footpath opposite the church named East Street. The track passes some garages on its way up to a farmhouse named Hey Meadow. Looking back there is an imposing view of Holcombe Moor and Peel Tower. Go through the nearest gate in the front garden of the farmhouse into the field beyond. Turn left to follow a fence, which skirts round the edge of the field above the farmhouse. Walk uphill to the top end of the field and climb over a wall stile. Turn left along a track for a distance of about 50 yards, and then turn right through a gate to follow another track named Sand Beds Lane.

Sand Beds Lane starts off in a cutting and ascends the slope of the hill. The track flattens out and on your left you pass an old derelict farmhouse. Where the track divides ignore the main track and take the right fork. The path now goes uphill through an overgrown cutting. After walking over a wooden fence continue along the path

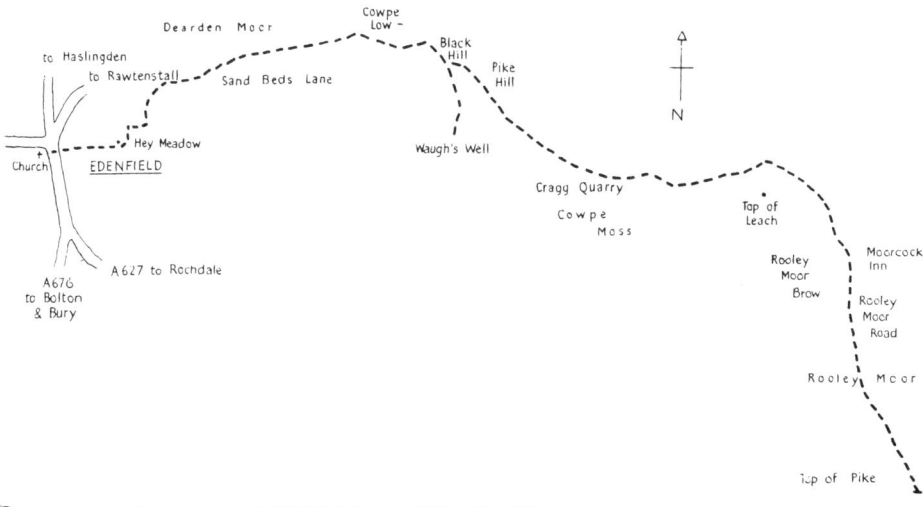

## Section 6 (Part): Edenfield to Top of Pike

## Section 6 (Part): Top of Pike to Whitworth Tonacliffe

## Section 7: Whitworth Tonacliffe to Wardle

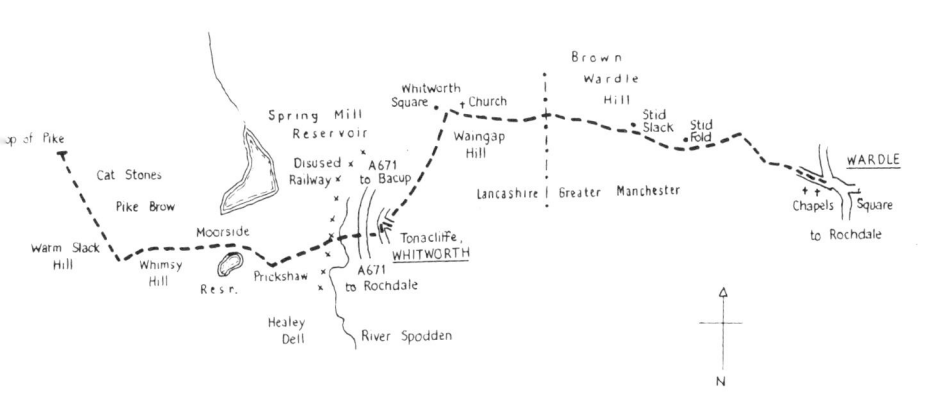

which merges with a track coming in from the left. Walk straight on to the top of the slope, where there are the first visible remains of the vast quarrying activities which took place during the last century. The track crosses an old stone bridge and if you glance below a stone walled cutting may be seen. The cutting was for the 3ft. narrow gauge railway from Clough Fold, Rawtenstall to Cragg and Ding Quarries. Turn right and walk parallel to the railway cutting. On your left is Cowpe Low, 1440ft (439m). The walking from here onwards is easier because of stone flags laid on the ground. In fact this was originally a quarry road and if you look carefully you can see grooves cut in to the stone, where carts and wagons once travelled. Presumably the road was superseded by the railway line during the nineteenth century.

The old road descends slightly to cross the former railway line and at this point there was once a level crossing, and remains of a bolt hole may be seen. The railway continues on your left, where an embankment can be seen. Further on the road meets the former railway again and near Black Hill there is a junction of several tracks. The direct route to Whitworth is straight on, but it is worth making the detour to Waugh's Well (details below).

Walk up the slope towards Cragg Quarry. The old spoil tips have been left for so long that they have almost blended into the landscape. The track continues along the edge of the hillside, where the view extends to Cowpe Reservoir and Rossendale valley. The occasional presence of trail riders is usually the only noise which you are likely to encounter in this isolated area. Continue at the same height in a general easterly direction until you merge with another track and walk in a south easterly direction. This is Rooley Moor Road, the old upland route between Rossendale and Rochdale. This is the highest part of the entire walk and the height is over 1500ft (465m). You are just below the summit of Top of Leach.

Follow Rooley Moor Road for a distance of about two miles. There are views of Knowl Hill and Naden Reservoirs to the west and the whalebacked shape of Brown Wardle Hill to the east. The road climbs over Top of Pike and descends about 150ft to Ordnance Survey spot height 1072ft (327m). Turn left along a track within 300 yards of an electricity transmission line. The track leads to the edge of Whimsy Hill. Walk over the edge of the hill and you can see Spring Mill Reservoir on your left and a smaller reservoir on your right. Whitworth and Healey Dell may also be seen in the distance. There is no path, but walk downhill across the moor in a general easterly direction to the left hand corner of Spring Mill Reservoir. Continue along a farm track until you reach the remains of Moorside Farm.

Walk to the right of a wall along a track with an electricity transmission line to your right. Go through a gate along a walled track. Walk alongside a row of derelict cottages and a farm-house named Prickshaw. Bear left at a T junction and turn left along a lane. Go through a gate on the right after 25 yards. Walk diagonally across a field underneath the electricity transmission line. There is no path here. Head for a gap in the wall at the far side of the field. It is interesting to note that stone flags are used for walling purposes here. Continue in the same easterly direction across another field and aim for a wooden gate, just to the left of the electricity transmission line. Bear left along a path which descends into the valley of Healey Dell. Cross the bridge over the track which leads to the A671 Rochdale and Rossendale road at Tonacliffe, a suburb of Whitworth. There is a seat, shelter and car park and buses run between Rochdale and Bacup (G.M.T.).

## Detour to Waugh's Well

The detour from the main route near Black Hill to Waugh's Well is less than a mile altogether and is well worth making. Turn right and walk in a southerly direction along a path beside the remains of an old wall, which merges with a track from the right. Walk along the track in the same direction. The old farmhouse at Fo' Edge has unfortunately been demolished but the foundations remain. Shortly afterwards you come to Waugh's Well. Return to the main route along the same track and path.

## Points of Interest:

**Waugh's Well.** The well was erected in 1866 to the memory of Edwin Waugh, the Lancashire dialect writer, who wrote extensively about the area. In addition to his dialect writing he produced some vivid accounts of the area in books such as 'Lancashire Sketches'. The Edwin Waugh Society was founded in his honour and an annual procession from Turn village to Waugh's Well is followed by readings of his work.

Edwin Waugh, nicknamed 'Nedd Waff', was born on 29th January 1817. He became a journeyman printer, although he preferred walking on the moors, writing and reading dialect verse and Lancashire history. His writings on the cotton famine brought him considerable fame and so his followers constructed the well at his favourite spot. Waugh reputedly spent more time walking, writing, reading and drinking than he did at home. One story tells of how he left home to let his wife and mother-in-law to do the spring cleaning. In the process they burnt his manuscripts. It is said that Waugh never returned home again!

The well has been renovated and rebuilt recently by Mr Baldwin and Mr Sagar of Rawtenstall. A bronze head of Waugh sculptured by Mrs Lord of Newchurch and Mr. Bonzor of Rochdale was incorporated into the structure; 450 people gathered to watch Harry Craven unveil the well on 16th July 1966. The well also contains two plaques. One is dedicated to the memory of Ward Ogden, a naturalist and rambler; the other plaque commemorates the work of Harry

Craven and is written by Harvey Kershaw: 'He left his mark on memory's page, By striving might and main, Th'owd dialect i' this modern age, To foster and sustain.'.

**Cragg Quarry.** The quarry was originally owned by Butterworth and Brooks and was one of numerous quarries in the area. Stone has been extracted from these hills from early times, although the industry reached its peak in the Victorian age, when stone was required for pavements and buildings in the fast growing towns and cities. Much of Trafalgar Square was built from local stone. The industry prospered until just after the end of the first world war, but nowadays there are only a few working quarries. The reasons for the decline of the industry were that the costs of transportation were high, several quarries had been worked out and were uneconomic, and the quarrymen were no longer willing to work for poor wages, when they had to face hard physical labour in harsh conditions. The area experiences severe weather conditions in the winter and originally men had to walk to and from work — a distance of over 5 miles, as the railway was designed to carry freight rather than passengers! In October 1920 Mrs Brooks sold the railway engines and equipment.

**Top of Leach.** A few hundred yards away from the route to your right is the summit of Top of Leach (1555 ft or 474m) where an hexagonal column marks the five townships of Bacup, Haslingden, part of Ramsbottom, Rawtenstall and Whitworth which comprise the borough of Rossendale.

**The Moorcock Inn.** This inn on Rooley Moor Road used to be a popular destination for walkers, and at 1325ft (404m) it was one of the highest inns in the country. It stood at Rooley Moor Brow, just south of the path from Ding Quarry. It ended its days during the second world war when the last landlord could not carry on after his son had 'joined up' and the licence lasped. The old inn became a target for artillery practice. At one time it was known as the 'North Eastern'.

**Rochdale and Bacup Railway.** The railway was constructed in 1865, principally to transport stone from local quarries to Rochdale and beyond. The passenger service was rarely profitable, mainly due to competition from the Manchester, Bury and Bacup railway and the Manchester to Bacup tramway and it closed on 16th June 1947, although freight trains carried coal between Rochdale and Whitworth until 1967. The trackbed has been put to good use as it now forms part of a nature trail through Healey Dell.

**Healey Dell.** Formed by the erosive action of the River Spodden cutting through sandstone and shale to create a moorland clough, in which woodlands and waterfalls and geological features combine to give a wide range of flora and fauna. In 1972 the local councils and naturalists combined to create Healey Dell Nature Reserve and a three mile long nature trail was officially opened in July 1972. There are many varieties of trees, grasses, and several species of birds, insects and microscopic plant life. Allan Marshall has produced a booklet about the flora and fauna and a leaflet about the nature trail has been published by Rochdale Field Naturalists in conjunction with Rochdale Council.

**Section 7**  **2 miles**

# Whitworth (Tonacliffe) to Wardle.

IN CONTRAST to the previous section the route heads across lower ground on the fringes of Rochdale. Several small farms remain and the fields are criss-crossed by a mass of paths and tracks. After passing Whitworth Church with its interesting gargoyles the walk follows one of the old roads to Wardle. Wardle Square is a conservation area and is dominated by two chapel buildings.

## Route:

Start from the A671 Rochdale and Rossendale road at Tonacliffe, a suburb of Whitworth (locally pronounced Whito'th), at the car park, shelter and substation. Cross the road and follow the public footpath sign opposite. The path runs between two rows of terraced houses. Walk up some steps to Tonacliffe Road. Walk across the road along Tonacliffe Way for a short distance before turning left to follow a path, keeping a school playground fence to your left. The path fords a shallow stream and continues in a northerly direction towards Whitworth Church, which may be seen in the distance. The path comes out opposite the church, and if you glance to the left Whitworth Square can be seen, once the home of the Whitworth Doctors.

Proceed uphill past the church in an easterly direction and walk past a golf club on your right. Follow a cobblestone track to the top of the slope. On your left is Brown Wardle Hill, a favourite spot for hang gliding enthusiasts. The route from here to Wardle is difficult to locate because of the mass of paths leading off in all directions. The lack of waymaking adds to the difficulties and the use of the 'South Pennines' 1:25 000 Leisure Map is suggested here. There are several different routes to Wardle, but the one described here is the most direct and traditionally used track. At the top of the slope there are five tracks leading off in different directions. Leave the tarmac road and turn left along the cinder track. After 20 yards there is a fork in the track and you should take the left fork and walk in an easterly direction towards Stid Slack farm. The track reaches the brow of a small hill and two gates can be seen in front of you. Go through the flag stile by the gate on the left; the nearest one of the stream, and walk past the fence in front of Stid Slack, which is on your left.

The footpath is indistinct but has been waymarked by a farmer. Go through a gate and continue to the next farm, Stid Fold, along a more distinct track. Before reaching the farm go through a gate, keep to the right of the farmhouse and walk to the left of the farm outbuildings. Now walk along a sunken track between field walls (or just above it) and pass through some more gates. Come out onto a metalled road after half a mile or so and walk straight on along the road. Continue over a flagged bridge in the direction of Wardle and walk past a row of weavers cottages and some new detached houses. Wardle House and Wardle Mill may both be seen before the road comes to the main square. From Wardle Square there is a good bus service to Rochdale (G.M.T.).

## Points of Interest:

**Whitworth Square.** The square was once the home of the Taylor family, known as the Whitworth Doctors. Today they might be dismissed as eccentric quacks, but in their time they were respected nationally and were held in high esteem as far away as Australia and New Zealand. Patients travelled from far and wide in search of treatment for a variety of different ailments. The Taylors were once farriers by trade, but James Taylor, who lived until 1752, discovered that he was able to treat horses successfully and used his cures on other animals before transferring his skills to humans. He and his descendents began to practice medicine at their surgery at Whitworth Square. The detached building at the end of the square was the hospital and the track from the square to the church was named the 'Cripples Walk'. The Doctors in common with customary medical practice did not believe in gentle or subtle forms of treatment and they reputedly 'bled their patients by the gallon and drugged them by the stone'. They frequently prescribed an embrocation entitled the 'Whitworth Red Bottle', and an anit-spasmodic tinture which contained herbs gathered from nearby woods and camphor called 'Whitworth Drops'.

John Taylor (1740-1802) was supposed to have paid a visit to Princess Elizabeth who complained of 'pain and stupor in the head'. Taylor ordered her to take his snuff, which he claimed had the property of 'Purging the head'. After she had taken the medicine the princess complained of continual sneezing. When Taylor was recalled to the court and told of this he smiled and said: 'Let the girl sneeze, that is the very thing that will do her good!' Apparently the princess was relieved of her complaint.

The Taylor family were willing to treat all patients regardless of how rich or poor they were and one cartoon shows the doctors leaving a bishop who was awaiting treatment for a tooth in order to treat a horse, which belonged to a local farmer. The last practising doctor was James Eastwood Taylor who died in 1876. Many members of the family are buried in the churchyard, as are some of the patients who failed to respond to treatment. Probably the Taylors' main achievement was their pioneering work in the field of bone setting and much of their knowledge was obtained from their work with animals.

**Whitworth Church (St. Bartholemew's).** St. Bartholemew's Church dates from 1847 and the foundation stone was laid by Doctor James Taylor of Todmorden

Hall. There are some interesting gargoyles on the outside walls depicting angels and lions as well as local figures such as the first choirmaster and vicar. There was some controversy over the building of the church, because it was originally intended to use Yorkshire stone in its construction. Local feelings ran high and the villagers threatened to boycott the church completely if Whitworth stone was not used. Their wishes were granted and stone from local quarries was used to build the church.

**Brown Wardle Hill.** The whaleback shape of Brown Wardle Hill is a landmark for several miles around. It is 1311ft (400m) high and on a clear day offers a view over Whitworth, Watergrove Reservoir and as far as Hollingworth Lake and Blackstone Edge. The Hill was used by neolithic man as a watchtower and remains of flint arrowheads and scrapers have been found there. Today it is a venue for hang gliding enthusiasts.

**Wardle.** Wardle Square contains a shop, a former branch co-operative building, a public house, which was formerly a packhorse inn, and two chapel buildings side by side. The two Wesleyan chapels were both built during the nineteenth century. The smaller building was built in 1809 and is now used as a scout headquarters, whilst the larger building dates from 1873 and was constructed to hold a bigger congregation. Both structures have been cleaned and act as a grandiose focal point of the square: a far cry from the days when the Methodists under John Wesley preached in the converted Wardle Fold Barn.

Section 8        3½ miles

# Wardle to Walsden (Bottoms Mill)

THE route returns to the moors after following the banks of Watergrove Reservoir and the hills mark a significant milestone in the journey since they form the county boundary between Greater Manchester (formerly Lancashire) and West Yorkshire. There is still rivalry between Lancastrians and Yorkshiremen to this day and each still claim their separate identities. Geographically there are changes too because this is the Pennine watershed and from here onwards streams no longer flow into the Mersey estuary and the Irish Sea. Instead they flow eastwards into the Humber estuary and the North Sea. After walking along the Long Causeway, an old packhorse route, the path descends to Calderdale and the section ends in a part of Walsden marked on the map as Bottoms.

## SECTION 8: WARDLE TO WALSDEN Bottoms Mill

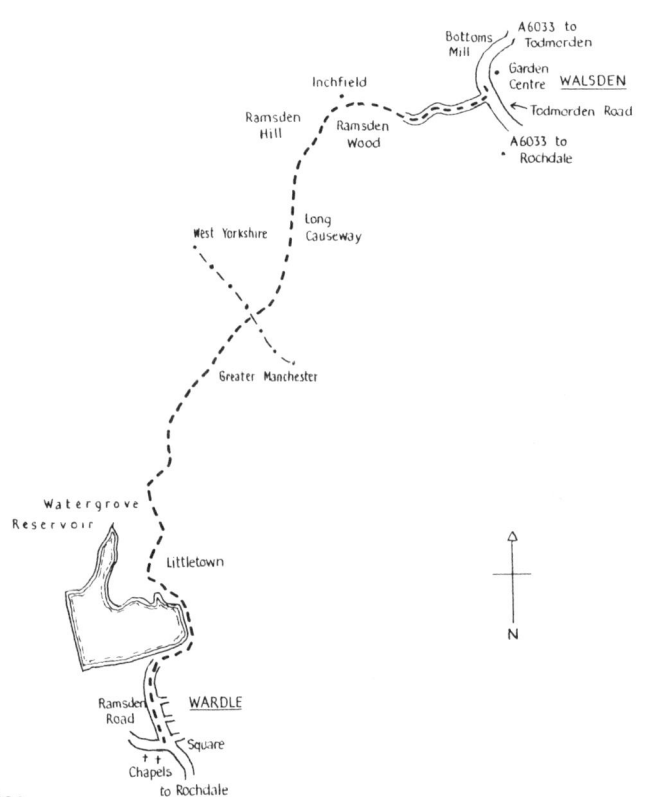

## Route:

Leave Wardle Square and walk in a northerly direction along Ramsden Road, past a seat built to commemorate the Silver Jubilee of Queen Elizabeth II and a road named Alderbank on your right. The road gives way to stone setts passing beneath an electricity transmission line and the remains of some terraced houses. Go through a gate which forms the entrance to Watergrove Reservoir. The old road used to go straight on at this point, but it has been diverted around the right side of the reservoir. Turn right to follow the wall on the south side of the reservoir, keeping the reservoir wall to your left at the lintel stones rescued from the old village of Watergrove and now embedded in the walls at the south-east corner of the reservoir. The track heads round the eastern side of the reservoir to its northern end, where the wall ceases. Do not go uphill yet but continue on the level track. The route continues along

Ramsden Road again. Further along the remains of the hamlet of Littletown are seen, with numerous old walls which are no longer used.

Continue in a northerly direction along Ramsden Road until you reach the point where the walls on either side of the track finish and open moorland is reached. Fork right after crossing a flag bridge and follow a faint track which climbs up the hill-side. The track is called the Long Causeway and is a former packhorse route which goes between Rough Hill and Crook Hill. Stone slabs marking the route can be seen half buried in the ground. Walk uphill past a small red spoil heap — a reminder of the mining on these hills. The track continues in a north-easterly direction and there are stone cairns on the side to guide you. There is a retrospective view of Brown Wardle Hill, Rochdale and the Manchester conurbation on this stretch of 'border country', and as the view recedes a new vista appears in front of you to the east. Stoodley Pike and its tower may be seen and below it the Calder Valley. Walk over a flag bridge and go through a gap in a dry stone wall.

The track descends slightly and follows a dry stone wall, which is on your right for some distance. Walk underneath an electricity transmission line and descend the slope and go through a metal gate. Turn left and join a track from a farm named North Ramsden Farm, which is on your left. The track becomes a metalled road and it passes two small ponds, owned by the Walsden Printing Company. Walk past the company's mill buildings, which are still in active use, and continue past the attractively situated mill cottages and streets known as Top Street and The Mullions. Continue along the road which descends through this beautiful moorland clough towards the Calder Valley. Walk past some newly built bungalows and terraced cottages. The road (Ramsden Wood Road) comes out at Todmorden Road, Walsden. Turn left along the A6033 Rochdale and Todmorden Road towards Bottoms Mill, near the garden centre, from where there is a regular bus service (W.Y).

## Points of Interest:

**Watergrove Reservoir.** The reservoir occupies the site of the old village of Watergrove which was evacuated in the late 1920s. The reservoir took eight years to build and was finally completed in April 1938. Some 40 farms also had to be evacuated, since they were within the gathering areas for the reservoir. It was a job creation project designed to provide employment for 500 men at time of unemployment. The stone for the walls was quarried locally and some of it came from the village of Watergrove.

Not far from here was the setting for the 'Simple Life Holiday Home' set up by Misses Macrae and Cave in July 1911. Their brochure advertised the house 'Mountain View' as being situated among the hills 'where the air is fresh and bracing.' In the brochure it said: 'Whilst reasonable comforts are provided no attempt will be made to imitate the attentions belonging to fashionable boarding establishments'. The diet was strictly home-grown and vegetarian. Among the attractions was a 'mountain stream' and two open air bathing ponds. Some of the visitors, even in a less permissive age than our own, took advantage of this facility and engaged in nude bathing. They were possibly encouraged by the promise that 'visitors have every freedom to use the facilities available'. The local people soon started gossiping about these 'strange goings on' and a local policeman called to tell the nude bathers to "stop it or else".

On the hills there are a number of spoil heaps from the mining activity that took place here. There are many 'breest heegh' (breast high) mines and during the 18th and 19th centuries farmers would supplement their income by mining as well as domestic weaving.

**Walsden.** Straggles the valley bottom following the A6033 Rochdale and Todmorden road. The name apparently means 'the valley of the Welsh'. A finger post on the corner of Ramsden Wood Road and Todmorden Road indicates that it is 7 miles from Rochdale and 2 miles from Todmoreden. The village contains shops, public houses and a fish shop. At the garden centre refreshments are available every day of the week. Regular bus services to Littleborough, Burnley, Todmorden and other Calderdale towns leave from near Bottoms Mill (W.Y.).

Section 9                                                               7 miles

# Walsden (Bottoms Mill) to Hebden Bridge

AT WALSDEN the canal towpath of the Rochdale Canal is encountered for the first time and after a short canalside walk the route leaves the valley and climbs to Warland Reservoir. Following the Pennine Way to Stoodley Pike there are views over Todmorden, Mankinholes and the Calder Valley. Leaving the Pennine Way at Kilnshaw Lane the walk passes Erringden Grange, once the centre of a hunting park, before reaching Crow Nest Wood, where excellent views of Hebden Bridge may be obtained. Descend through the woods to Hebden Bridge, commonly known as the South Pennine Centre, where split-level terraced housing clings to the steep hillsides.

## Route:

From Bottoms Mill at Walsden walk in a northerly direction along Todmorden Road, the A6033 Rochdale and Todmorden Road. Walk over a railway bridge and turn right to follow the towpath of the Rochdale Canal. Walk in a southerly direction for about ¾ mile to the county boundary at Warland. Four locks and three bridges are passed. After the third bridge and fourth disused lock there is a row of cottages which back directly onto the canal towpath. Walk under a bridge and pass alongside another bridge and weir. On your left there is a view of an unusual turreted wall of Warland Farm. Turn right towards Warland across the next bridge, a wooden bridge, and carry straight on past Woodbank House.

Walk uphill along a roughly metalled track past Claremont Terrace, a split-level terrace, and past Warland Farm, dated 1665. Turn sharp right by the gable end of the terrace and continue up the metalled track past another cottage. Further on go through a gate and follow the waterworks road. Bear right and walk past a new waterworks cottage and pumping station. Turn right in front of an old farmhouse. Go through two gates within 200 yards of each other and continue walking uphill keeping parallel to a stream. Climb the slope to the edge of Warland reservoir and turn left at the top along the waterworks road which now forms part of the Pennine Way.

At the northern end of Warland Reservoir follow the track beside Warland Drain for ½ mile. There is now another view of Stoodley Pike at Langfield Common. The route here is well marked with cairns and parish boundary stones. After passing the small rounded mound of Coldwell Hill, descend Bald Scout Hill until you reach Withins Gate, near height 1208ft(368m). For those who wish to descend to Mankinholes turn left along a path known as the 'Long Drag' or 'Long Stoup', which is a paved way to the village, where there is a youth hostel.

The path continues in the same north-easterly direction towards Stoodley Pike following the edge of the hillside. Stoodley Pike obelisk contains stairs to a gallery from where fine views may be obtained. From the Pike walk in an easterly direction until you come to a gap stile. About 40 yards further on the path turns left over a wall stile and descends the hill. When you reach Kilnshaw Lane, a bridleway, the route parts company with the Pennine Way, so instead of going straight on, turn right and walk on the bridleway. Walk along Kilnshaw Lane for about ¾ mile past some farmhouses named Swillington, Mitton, Kilnshaw Farm and Erringden Grange. You are now on a plateau above the Calder Valley and directly opposite you on the other side of the valley is the village and church of Heptonstall.

Carry straight on at a crossroads of tracks and then turn left to walk along the signposted path to Old Chamber. Descend slightly and

## SECTION 9: WALSDEN Bottoms Mill TO HEBDEN BRIDGE

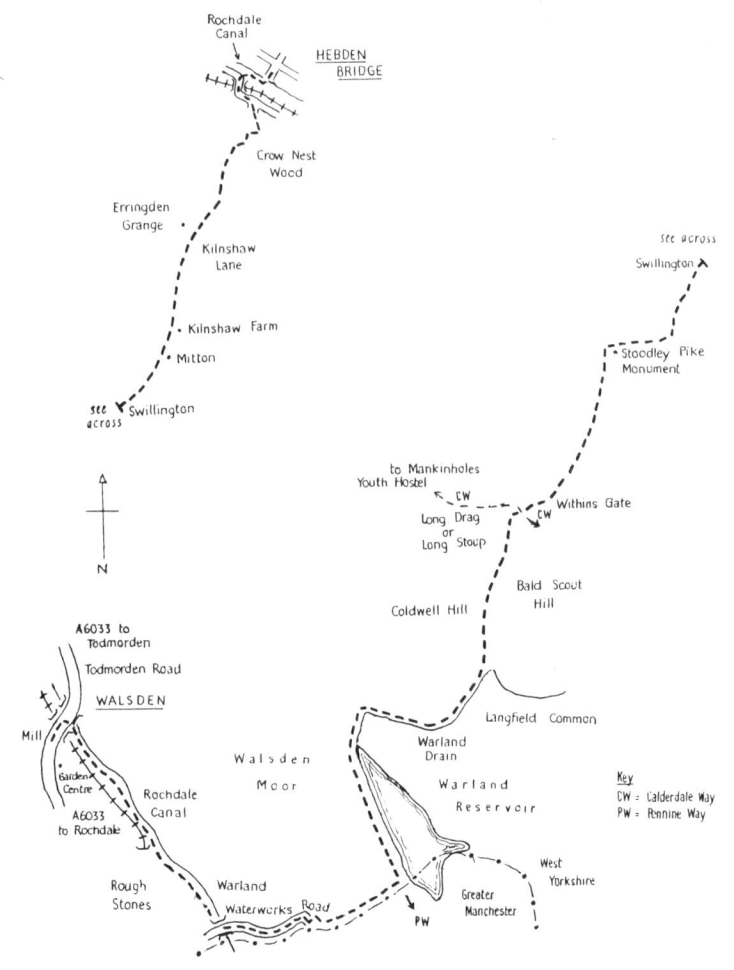

again carry straight on at a second junction of tracks. From here the steep hillsides of Hebden Bridge may be seen in the distance The path veers right and goes downhill to pass underneath a stone bridge — an early and unusual 'walkers' underpass'! Continue descending the slope to enter Crow Nest Wood. The path zig-zags downhill through the wood. The path turns left and then joins a more distinct path near a wooden gate. Turn right down this track, and when it forks, take the left fork. The track leads downhill into Park View, Fairfield, a suburb of Hebden Bridge.

If you intend catching a train from Hebden Bridge turn right along Park View and Palace House Road. Turn left to the railway station, which is signposted. For those walking to the centre of the town, turn left along Park View and cross the railway bridge. About 50 yards further on leave the road and turn right down a set of five steps and follow a track. Take the first turning on the left and walk down some more steps to a path beside the Rochdale Canal. The path crosses an aqueduct over the River Calder. Turn left and walk over the canal bridge above the disused Black Pit Lock and walk along Holme Street. After passing a school and a post office, you come out onto the A646 Burnley and Halifax Road at New Road, where there are bus stops for several destinations. On the opposite side of the road, however, is the Tourist Information Centre, at 1, Bridge Gate. The centre is open seven days a week all through the year. Literature on the South Pennine area may be obtained in addition to exhibitions by local artists and details of accommodation and other information. (Telephone 843831).

## Points of Interest

**The Rochdale Canal.** The canal was completed in 1804 and was used for transporting cotton, machinery, flour, coal and other commodities across the Pennines. The canal was a great engineering feat in a hostile environment. It is 33 miles long and links Manchester and Sowerby Bridge. The canal has 92 locks, more for the distance than any other canal in the Kingdom. It was calculated that each boat would require 165,000 gallons to cross the Pennines and so six reservoirs were built. (One of these, Warland Reservoir, is visited on the walk). Canal travel was not as slow as we might imagine — 30 or 40 tons of cloth would leave Todmorden at about 6.0 pm and would be delivered in Manchester early next morning. The canal was initially very profitable and the volume of traffic rose to 50 boats per day in 1888. In the long run, however, it was not able to compete successfully with the railway and road and has fallen into disuse this century. The last boat to make the full journey went through in June 1939. Ironically, the railway engines made by George Stephenson in Newcastle were transported across the Pennines by the canal that would eventually be displaced by the railways! Today, the Rochdale Canal Society aim eventually to restore the canal for recreation and pleasure purposes.

**The Manchester and Leeds Railway.** This was another major engineering achievement and was the first ever Trans-Pennine rail link. The main obstacle on the route was the Summit Pass and so a tunnel was necessary. It took two years to construct the Summit Tunnel under the Pennine watershed, because of unexpected difficulties with the underground water deposits and rock faults. When completed in 1841 it was the longest rail tunnel in the world. The building costs were high and some £250,000 was spent on its construction. The line was opened on 1st March 1841 and George Stephenson was one of the first passengers to ride underneath the Pennines. In those days the 1st class fare between Manchester and Leeds was 15 shillings (75p) for a 2¾ hour journey, compared with 12 shillings (60p) inside and 8 shillings (40p) outside for a stage coach ride of 3¾ hours. The railway runs side by side with the canal for much of the way between Littleborough and Sowerby Bridge, and the road is not far away, owing to the scarcity of level ground in the valley. The railway still carries passengers and freight traffic.

**The Pennine Way.** This is the best known long distance footpath in England and Wales. Originally conceived by Tom Stephenson in 1935, the path goes between Edale in Derbyshire and Kirk Yetholm in Scotland, a distance of over 250 miles.

**The 'Long Drag' or 'Long Stoup'.** There is a sad history attached to this path which crosses the walk near Withins Gate. During the cotton famine in the mid-nineteenth century there was no work and some families were close to starvation.The local industrialist, John Fielden, who lived at Dobroyd Castle, offered to pay mill workers for building a path between Mankinholes and his shooting lodge near Cragg Vale. The stone steps can still be seen and this is a good walking route to Mankinholes, where there is a youth hostel and a public house. It is here that the walk crosses the Calderdale Way for the first time.

**The Calderdale Way.** Britain's first official medium distance footpath was opened in October 1978, and the 50 mile circular route goes through the West Yorkshire Pennines linking moors, woods, farms, villages and towns. The Calderdale Way Association has waymarked and maintained the route and a booklet is available on the walk.

**Stoodley Pike.** Stoodley Pike is a 120 foot high obelisk, situated at 1310 feet (399m) above sea level. It is suggested that there may have been a warning beacon on the hill during the Spanish Armada. There was almost certainly a structure there before 1814, when a monument to commemorate the surrender of Paris to the Allies was built. Since then other developments appear to have coincided with world events. The building was completed at the time of the Battle of Waterloo in 1815; it collapsed in February 1854, on the same afternoon that the Russian Ambassador left London before the declaration of the Crimean War. The present structure was built in 1856, when peace with Russia was proclaimed; and on the morning of 11th November 1918, there was a partial collapse a few hours before peace was declared to end the First World War. On the structure is an 84 word inscription which stresses that it is not a traditional war memorial but a monument to peace. There is a gallery running round the monument at a height of 40 feet, reached by a flight of 39 steps.

**Erringden Grange.** This was once the home of sport for noblemen during the 12th and 13th centuries. Erringden was enclosed as a hunting park, where wild boars, deer, wolves and hares roamed. The owners of the hunting park were the Warenn family and they imposed harsh penalties on anyone found poaching or stealing wood, ferns or dry brushwood. In 1307 Dominus Roger, vicar of Rochdale, was fined a sum of £20 for poaching — obviously a huge sum of money then! In 1347 the Warenn family died out and the property reverted to the Crown, which did not bother to penalise people for poaching. The local inhabitants therefore poached freely without fear of punishment and they did so in earnest. In 1980 there were efforts to re-establish deer in the park.

**Hebden Bridge.** This is the largest settlement which is visited on the route and the town is an industrial and tourist centre. It formed a river crossing for the packhorse routes that made use of the Upper Calder valley. In 1508 William Greenwood bequeathed a sum of 13s 4d (67p) to build a stone bridge across the river. The bridge became a convenient meeting place for travellers and inns were built to serve their needs. The building of a turnpike road and the construction of West End Bridge vastly improved communications, and the Rochdale Canal and Manchester and Leeds Railway led to further growth. Fustian and corduroy clothing was the main industry and at Nutclough Mill the weavers formed the first co-operative. The Victorians built a number of 'top and bottom' (split-level) houses on the steep hillsides for mill-workers and they contribute towards a unique urban environment. The Tourist Centre at 1, Bridge Street sells a self-guided walk, 'The Hebden Bridge Trail', produced by the Calder Civic Trust, as well as other information about this fascinating town. There is a good bus service to Burnley, Halifax and other Calderdale towns. There is a weekend service to Haworth (W.Y.).

## Section 10                                                    1½ miles

# Hebden Bridge to Midge Hole (New Bridge)

THERE are several features of interest on this very short section. The route leaves Hebden Bridge and climbs to the side of Hell Hole Rocks, which overlook the Calder Valley. It is not far to the hilltop village of Heptonstall where the two churches, Methodist chapel and museum are all worth a visit. The path goes downhill past North Well and through Lee Wood to Midge Hole, the entrance to Hardcastle Crags.

## Route

Starting from outside the Tourist Information Office at West End, Hebden Bridge, cross West Street and walk past the former Ebenezer Chapel, now the Art Centre. After walking past the junction with Hebble End, turn right along a cobbled path known as Stoney Lane. The path goes uphill in a series of steps past some three storey terraces on your right. At the top of the steps turn right along Heptonstall Road. Walk past Lee Royd and Queens Terrace and turn left along a signposted footpath to Hell Hole Rocks and Heptonstall. After about 50 yards take the right fork along the track which leads uphill. Whilst ascending the slope take a look at the view over Hebden Bridge and the Calder Valley, which are now a considerable distance below the path.

SECTIONS 9 & 10:
   The route through HEBDEN BRIDGE

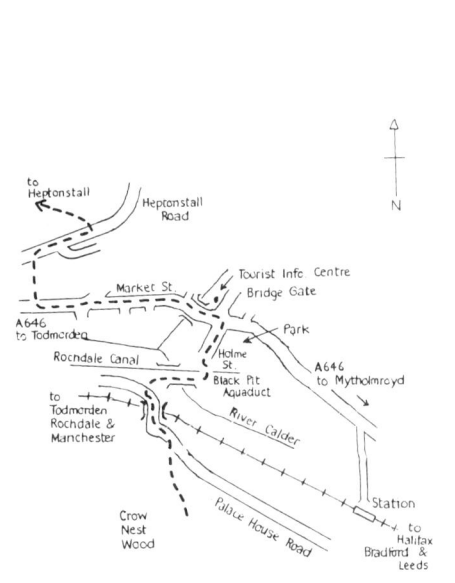

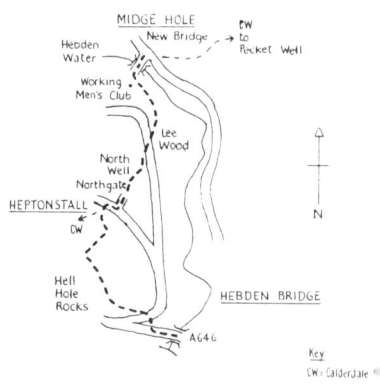

## SECTION 10: HEBDEN BRIDGE TO MIDGE HOLE New Bridge

Further along is a disused quarry known as Hell Hole Rocks. The path leaves the edge of the hillside and ascends the slope at the left of the rockface by means of a series of steps cut into the rock. At the top is a stone wall. At this point your route joins the Calderdale Way route. Turn sharp right along a walled track leading into Heptonstall. This is Eaves Lane. At the end of the lane bear left and walk behind some modern houses. Bear right and walk along West Laithe, which contains some historic buildings including Chantry House. After passing Chantry House on your left go through Dog Lane Gate up the steps into the churchyard. Turn right through the church gates, with the museum on your right and the old church on your left. Pass through Great North Gate with the Cloth Hall on your left to reach Towngate. Turn right along Towngate and then turn left by the "Cross Inn' Public House into Northgate.

Walk along Northgate past Whitehall Arch, a high lintel, on your left and the Methodist Chapel on your right. Fork right just before reaching the remains of some stocks which are 10 yards to your left near the appropriately named Stocks Villas. Leave Heptonstall by walking along an old packhorse route to Haworth, Northwell Lane, which descends to join a track at the gates of North Well House. The track comes out at Lee Wood Road, where there is an old finger signpost, a seat and a bus stop (W.Y.). Cross the road and walk in the same direction to Hebden Dale. Looking up from the woods the War Memorial at Pecket Well may be seen in the distance. Walk straight on at a crossroads of paths. Further on is Midge Hole Working Mens' Club on your left. Locally known as 'Blue Pig' after its strange weathervane it is surely one of the most idyllic locations for such a building! Turn right to cross New Bridge over Hebden Water and pass a row of cottages, where you part company with the Calderdale Way. Midge Hole is the entrance to Hardcastle Crags and it contains a car park.

For those wishing to finish the walk here and wanting to make a circular walk back to Hebden Bridge there are a few possibilities. The road from Midge Hole leads to Hebden Bridge. A walk through Crimsworth Wood is an alternative route and this leads to Pecket Well, from where there are bus services to Hebden Bridge (W.Y.).

## Points of Interest:

**Heptonstall.** The township of Heptonstall was mentioned in the Domesday Survey and in early times the population were involved in both hand-loom weaving and agriculture, since the land was not sufficiently fertile for profitable farming alone. The prosperity of the township did not survive industrialisation, because mills and transportation networks developed in valley settlements such as nearby Hebden Bridge rather than on the hilltops. Heptonstall has been well preserved and is now a conservation area.

There is much to see in Heptonstall including the two churches, the Methodist Chapel and the Old Grammar School (now a museum). Heptonstall has two Anglican churches, built side by side — a rare feature in Britain. The older church, which is ruined, dates from probably earlier than 1256 and was dedicated to St. Thomas Becket. The churchyard contains the grave of 'King David' Hartley, one of the Cragg Vale coiners who produced counterfeit money.

Other buildings of interest include the reputedly haunted Chantry House, in West Laithe, where the bones of the dead were once stored and the Old Grammar School in Church Lane, built from a legacy provided from the Reverend Charles Greenwood. This is now a museum of village history and is open on most weekends. Along Northgate there are some old carvings inscribed on some of the buildings. One inscription on New House is dated 1736 and shows two figures: Henry and Elizabeth Foster. There is also a high lintel dated 1578 carrying the initials I.B., and this is known as Whitehall Arch. On the other side of Northgate is almost certainly the oldest Methodist chapel still in active use today. The octagonal shaped building dates from 1764 and its foundation stone was laid by John Wesley.

An excellent and reasonably priced 'Heptonstall Trail' guide has been published by the Calder Civic Trust and is available from information centres and local shops.

# Section 11　　　　　　　　　　　　　　　11 miles

# Midge Hole (New Bridge) to Haworth

THE final section of the walk takes you into the heart of Brontë Country, but first there is an easy stroll through the deeply wooded Hebden Valley and Hardcastle Crags. At Blake Dean the landscape changes and the moorlands can be seen. After rejoining the Pennine Way the route passes the reservoir at Walshaw Dean before ascending Withins Height, the last great moorland top on the walk. From here Top Withins may be seen, commonly believed to be the 'Wuthering Heights' of Emily Brontë. After passing Top Withins the walk parts company with the Pennine Way and descends to Brontë Bridge and Falls which also have connections with the famous family. A moorland walk through Penistone Hill Country Park brings you to the edge of Haworth. Finally a wooded track leads you into Haworth Churchyard and emerges at the top of Haworth village.

## Route

Walk past the car park at Midge Hole which forms the entrance to Hebden Valley and Hardcastle Crags. Either keep to the main track or bear left after the car park to follow the riverside path. Both routes converge at Gibson Mill, another relic of the industrial revolution situated in the middle of the woodlands. Turn left at Gibson Mill over an old toll bridge and turn right to follow the opposite bank of Hebden Water. The path passes some ponds which were once attached to the mill. At High Greenwood Wood leave the river bank and fork left along a well defined track, which gradually ascends the slope in a north to north-westerly direction. The track reaches the top of the slope and flattens out. Walshaw may be seen across the valley.

Go straight on and ignore a path forking off to the right. Keeping a wall to your left walk past Hell Holes, a quarry which provided stone for the nearby reservoirs. Leaving the woods continue in the same direction parallel to Hebden Water. The trestles of the old railway to Walshaw Dean Reservoir may be seen in the valley below. The path comes out on the Hebden Bridge and Widdop road. Turn right and follow the road to Blake Dean.

Walk across Blake Dean Bridge and go through a gap on the left-hand side of the gates to follow a waterworks track to Walshaw Dean Reservoirs. The track runs in a north-westerly direction parallel to Alcomden Water. Further on the Pennine Way track joins the route, which then descends to the water board house between

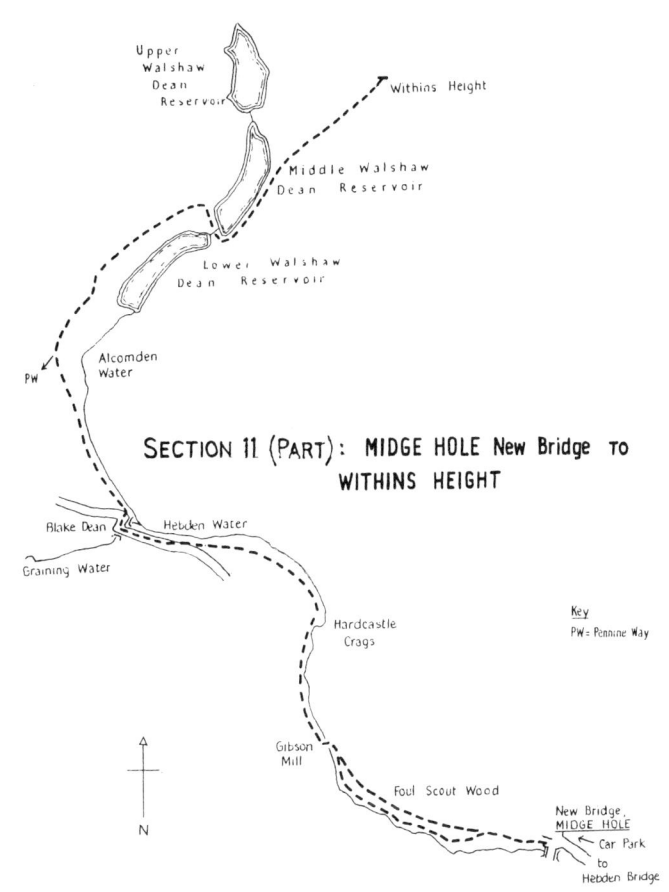

**SECTION 11 (PART): MIDGE HOLE New Bridge TO WITHINS HEIGHT**

Key
PW = Pennine Way

Lower and Middle Walshaw Dean Reservoirs. Cross the reservoir dam and on the opposite side of the reservoir turn left and walk beside the reservoir drain of Middle Walshaw Reservoir. Cross a stream known as Black Clough and go through a gate. A path ascends Withins Height and you pass 'Willkinson's Monument', dedicated to the memory of E. Wilkinson, a rambler. You may also encounter a stone, on which an advertisement for Ponden Hall has been placed — such is the popularity of the Pennine Way. The path reaches a height of about 1475ft (450m), although it does not quite go to the summit of Withins Height. There are fine views across West Yorkshire and as you descend from Withins Height an old farmhouse comes into view. This is no ordinary farmhouse: it is the remains of Top Withins, which is reputedly the setting for Emily Brontë's 'Wuthering Heights'.

Shortly after Top Withins you reach the remains of Middle Withins and from here there is a waymarked path to Brontë Bridge. The route parts company with the Pennine Way and bears right to run above the north side of South Dean Beck. It eventually descends to the beck at

## SECTION 11 (PART): WITHINS HEIGHT TO HAWORTH

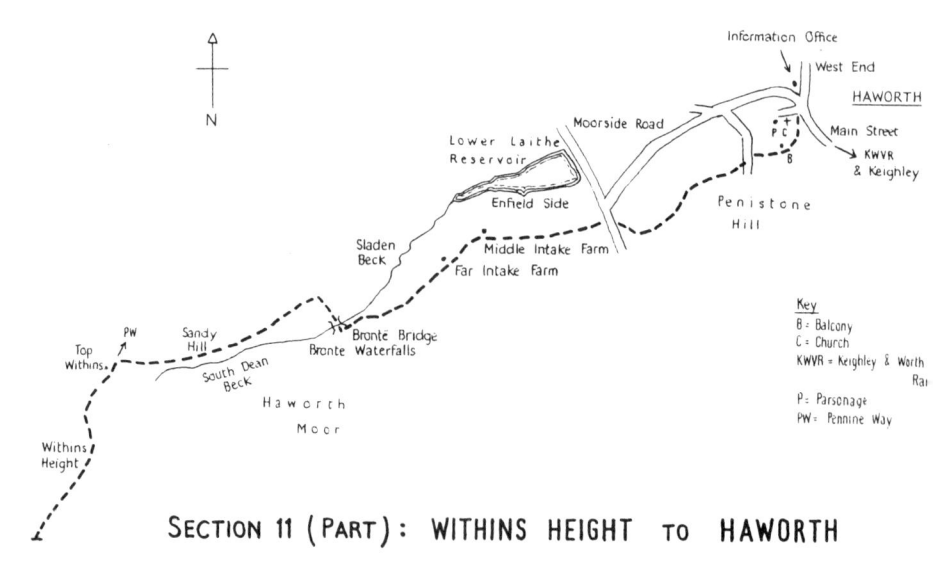

Brontë Bridge. Walk over the bridge and glance at Brontë Falls and Charlotte's Chair. A psalm has been inserted on one of the rocks here.

Turn left at Brontë Bridge and follow a track past two derelict intake farms — Far Intake and Middle Intake Farms. The track comes out at a road junction. Turn right and walk along the road (Moorside Lane). After 100 yards bear left and walk across Penistone Hill Country Park to the ranger service caravan. Turn left and follow the signposted path to Haworth across a car park and the moorland below an Ordance Survey triangulation point. There is a good view of Lower Laithe Reservoir and Stanbury across the valley. At the first junction of paths go straight on and at the second junction of paths bear left and walk downhill to a metalled road.

The final lap of the walk involves crossing the road and following the signposted lane to 'Haworth Church'. It leads past Balcony farmhouse and soon afterwards turns left. To the right is a view over the roof-tops of the houses in Haworth reminding you that it is not far to go. Walk past some allotments and go through a kissing gate. You are now in Haworth churchyard. Turn left along a flagged path which takes you to a small lane. The Brontë Parsonage Museum is on your left and the Information Centre and village are on your right. Turn right and walk to the Information Centre at the junction of West Lane and Change Gate at the top of Main Street. This is the end the of walk, although there is much to see in Haworth.

# Points of Interest

**Hebden Dale and Hardcastle Crags.** This beautiful wooded area contains a variety of deciduous and evergreen trees and was handed over to the National Trust in 1951. A booklet produced by E. W. Watson of the Calder Civic Trust gives details of the 'Slurring Rock Nature Trail' which goes through the valley. On the main track to Gibson Mill there are rocks carrying plaques to Mr. Dent Sutcliffe and Mr. Walter Greaves, members of the Hebden Bridge Literary and Scientific Society. The track passes a wishing well, shelter and a clearing known as Rom Folly, which was formerly an old charcoal hearth. Shackleton's plantation nearby was the location for recent replanting of pine, spruce, larch, beech, sycamore, oak and ash. On the riverside path to Gibson Mill you pass a weir and the remains of New Bridge Mill, where water was diverted to provide power for driving a water wheel.

**Gibson Mill.** This monument to the industrial revolution is one of the best preserved local water-driven cotton mills. It was built in about 1800 and records of the working conditions in the mill during the early 19th century by the Factories Inquiries Commission tell of an average 72 hour week for the 21 workers employed there in 1833. Children were employed here and 10 and 11 year olds were paid a mere 2s 6d (12½p) per week, in comparison with the adult wage of 17 shillings (85p). Wages were lower than in the Lancashire cotton towns, although the owners were regarded as being very progressive when they abolished corporal punishment at a time when other mills kept children working hard by threatening to administer the strap for those seen to be avoiding work! Gibson Mill was converted to steam power about 1860, but closed down as a cotton spinning mill at the turn of the century. It has since had many other uses, including being used as a restaurant, roller skating rink and as a store for the boy scouts. Its woodland setting reminds you that not all early industry developed in the large towns, and that this is no dark satanic mill! The old toll bridge sign informs you that it cost horses and cows one penny and sheep a half-penny for the privilege of crossing the river at this point!

**Blake Dean and Walshaw Dean Reservoirs.** Blake Dean is situated at the meeting place of two streams — Alcomden Water and Graining Water — and it is a popular spot for day trippers during the summer months. Blake Dean Baptist Chapel was built in 1820, but has unfortunately been demolished. Nearby are the remains of a 700 feet long and 105 feet high wooden trestle bridge, which carried a 3 foot gauge railway from Whitehill Nook, below Heptonstall, to Walshaw Dean Reservoirs. The reservoirs, which are seen further on, were built between 1900 and 1907 to supply Halifax with water, and the railway transported materials over the hilly terrain. Whitehill Nook became a township for the navvies employed for its construction. It was nicknamed 'Dawson City', not after the original Klondike goldmines but after the name of one of the foremen. The men travelled to work in trucks and old Liverpool horse trams, with locomotives provided at both ends of the train. After the work had been completed local people used the bridge to walk across the valley, but after a fatal accident it was demolished in 1912, since it had no further economic use. The foundations, however, still provide a popular picnic site.

**Top Withins.** An old intake farmhouse usually taken to be the setting for the Earnshaw home in Emily Brontë's 'Wuthering Heights'. The name is appropriate and it is a magnificent moorland scene, although it is by no means certain that it was the true location for the building. In most people's minds, there is little doubt and thousands make the trek to visit the desolate ruined building. In 1964 the Brontë Society put up a plaque on the walls of the building saying: 'This farmhouse has been associated with "Wuthering Heights". The Earnshaw Home in Emily Brontë's novel. The buildings even when complete bore no resemblance to the house she described, but the situation may well have been in her mind, when she wrote of the moorland setting of the Heights. This plaque has been placed here in response to many inquiries'. Attempts have been made to restore the building, but the weather has taken its toll, and the local water authority has frowned upon the idea of restoring it, since it lies in the water gathering grounds for its reservoirs, although a small shelter has been placed on one side of the building. Top Withins can either mean 'Top Willows' or an old local dialect word meaning 'gap', although the trees around the building are sycamore trees.

**Brontë Bridge, Charlotte's Chair and Brontë Falls.** Brontë lovers flock to this spot, where there is a stone bridge across the beck, some rocks including Charlotte's Chair, and Brontë Falls, a waterfall which is seen to best advantage after a spate of heavy rain. There is an unhappy story attached to this place, associated with Charlotte Brontë's final walk on these moors. She was accompanied by her husband, the Reverend Arthur Nichols, on a walk from Haworth. She wrote: 'We set off not intending to go far, but though wild and cloudy it was fair in the morning. When we had got about half a mile on the moors Arthur suggested the idea of a waterfall. After the melted snow he said it would be fine. I had often wished to see it in its Winter power so we walked on. It was fine indeed; a perfect torrent racing over rocks, white and beautiful. It began to rain while we were watching it, and we returned home under a streaming sky. However, I enjoyed the walk inexpressibly and would not have missed the spectacle on any account ... '.Charlotte got very wet and later developed a severe chill, which deteriorated into a more serious condition. A few months later she died.

**Penistone Hill Country Park.** The West Yorkshire County Council have restored the 177 acre site of a former quarry and this moorland edge is now a Country park. Information services, car parks, rangers, waymarked footpaths and bridleways have been provided. There is an excellent view across the valley to Stanbury and beyond.

**Haworth.** Nowadays a major tourist centre, which is known for its steep main street paved with stone setts, its shops selling Brontë souvenirs, cafes, public houses and a preserved steam railway. There is a youth hostel on the opposite side of the village and other accommodation is available. The railway line goes to Keighley (K.W.V.R.) and the B.R. main line, and buses operate on a frequent service to Keighley, Halifax, Bradford and to other West Yorkshire towns. (W.Y. and W.Y.R.). The village owes its fame to the Brontës, but there have been other colourful characters here. It was a centre for non-conformism and was the home of the Reverend William Grimshaw, a fiery preacher who accompanied John

Wesley on his travels and helped to spread the message of Methodism to these parts. His methods of conversion were unorthodox, and during services he used to leave chapel to visit the public houses nearby. He used to threaten drinkers with a whip and eternal damnation if they did not accompany him back to chapel!

It is estimated that over a quarter of a million people visit Haworth each year to see the home of the Brontë sisters. In their tragically short lives they wrote some of the finest literature in the language. Charlotte wrote 'Jane Eyre', 'Shirley', 'Villette' and 'The Professor'; Emily wrote 'Wuthering Heights'; and Anne wrote 'Agnes Grey' and 'The Tennant of Wildfell Hall'; all were written between 1846 and 1853. The Brontë family moved to Haworth in 1820; Bramwell lived from 1817 to 1848; Emily from 1818 to 1848; Anne from 1820 to 1849; and Charlotte from 1816 to 1855. They were all outlived by their father Patrick Brontë who survived until. 1861. Since then the importance of their work has been recognised and even at the end of the last century tourists came to see the village where the Brontës lived. Although the church and parsonage have been altered since the death of the Brontës, much of the village has remained substantially unaltered and the parsonage has been turned into a museum by the Brontë Society to commemorate the sisters and their work.

The grave of Miss Lily Cove, Britain's first balloonist and parachutist, can be seen in Haworth Cemetary. She died whilst giving an exhibition performance in 1911 when she became detached from her parachute. The grave, which overlooks the venue of her final performance, is carved with a picture of a balloon.

The privately owned Keighley and Worth Valley Steam Railway is a restored 5 mile line with stations at Keighley, Ingrow, Damems, Oakworth, Haworth and Oxenhope. A vast collection of locomotives and rolling stock may be seen at the Railway Exhibition Yard next to the station at the bottom of the hill. The railway featured in the films 'The Railway Children' and 'Yanks'. Services operate every weekend and bank hoilidays and daily during July and August.

That then is the route across the Pennines. Although Brontë country is visited by thousands of people every year much of the route is off the beaten track and goes through lesser known, but equally attractive scenery. I hope that you have enjoyed doing the walk as much as I have. Alas there are no free pints of beer or badges or certificates to show that you have completed the walk; only the satisfaction that you have walked across the Pennines from Lancashire to Yorkshire and seen some beautiful northern scenery.

# Further Reading

### 1. West Pennine Moors (Adlington to Holcombe Brook).
Birtill, George (1966). *The Enchanted Hills,* Guardian Press, Chorley.
Birtill, George (1972). *The Hiker's Book of Rivington,* Guardian Press, Chorley.
Birtill, George (1976). *Heather in my Hat,* Nelson Press, Chorley.
Buck, G. R. (1982). *Walking in the Lancashire Pennines,* Dalesman, Clapham.
Cresswell, Michael *Bolton Boundary Walk,* Bolton Council, Bolton.
Hesketh, Phoebe (1972). *Rivington – The Story of a Village,* Peter Davies. London.
Rawlinson, John (1969). *About Rivington.* Nelson, Chorley.
Sellars, Gladys (1979). *Walks on the West Pennine Moors,* Cicerone Press, Preston.

### 2. Rossendale and Surrounding Areas (Holcombe Brook to Wardle).
Aspin, C. and Pilkington, D. (Ed.) (1977). *Helmshore,* Helmshore Local History. Society, Helmshore.
Bowden, K. F. (Ed.) (1975). *A Second Bacup Miscellany,* Lancashire County Council Library and Leisure Committee, Preston.
Marshall, Allan (1976). *Healey Dell,* Lancashire Naturalists Trust, Chorley.
Metropolitan Borough of Bury, Dept. of Planning and Architecture (1981). *Historic Trails: Holcombe*

### 3. West Yorkshire and Surrounding Areas (Wardle to Haworth).
Calder Civic Trust (1973). *Pennine Walks around Hebden Bridge,* Ridings Publishing Company, Driffield.
Calder Civic Trust (1979). *Hebden Bridge Trail.*
Calder Civic Trust (1981) *Heptonstall Trail.*
Calderdale Way Association with West Yorkshire Metropolitan County Council (1979). *The Calderdale Way.*
*Collins, Herbert (1974).* South Pennine Park, Dalesman, Clapham.
Mitchell, W. R. (1967). *Haworth and The Brontës,* Dalesman, Clapham.
Savage, E. M. (1974). *Stoodley Pike,* Todmorden Antiquarian Society, Todmorden.
Speakman, Colin (1982). *Wayfarer Walks in the South Pennines,* Dalesman & West Yorkshire P.T.E, Clapham.
Stephenson, Tom (1969). *The Pennine Way,* H.M.S.O., London.
Thompson, Clifford (1979). *Walking in the South Pennines,* Dalesman, Clapham.
Wainwright, A. (1968). *Pennine Way Companion,* Westmorland Gazette, Kendal.
Walker, Colin (1974). *A Walker on the Pennine Way-Section II: Standedge to Ponden,* Pendyke, Leamington.
Watson, E. W. *Slurring Rock Nature Trail,* Metropolitan Borough of Calderdale, Halifax